W9-CDT-209

The Best Keywords
for Resumes, Letters,
and Interviews

Powerful Words and Phrases for Landing Great Jobs!

Second Edition

Wendy S. Enelow, CCM, MRW, JCTC, CPRW
Louise Kursmark, CCM, MRW, JCTC, CPRW

IMPACT PUBLICATIONS
Manassas Park, VA

Copyright © 2016 by Wendy S. Enelow and Louise Kursmark. All rights reserved. Printed in the United States of America. No part of this book may be used or reproduced in any manner whatsoever without written permission of the publisher: IMPACT PUBLICATIONS, 9104 Manassas Drive, Suite N, Manassas Park, VA 20111, Tel. 703-361-7300 or Fax 703-335-9486.

Second Edition: First edition, by Wendy S. Enelow, published as *Best KeyWords for Resumes, Cover Letters, and Interviews* (ISBN 978-1-57023-195-7) in 2003

Warning/Liability/Warranty: The authors and publisher have made every attempt to provide the reader with accurate, timely, and useful information. However, given the rapid changes taking place in today's economy and job market, some of this information will inevitably change. The information presented here is for reference purposes only. The authors and publisher make no claims that using this information will guarantee the reader job or career success. The authors and publisher shall not be liable for any losses or damages incurred in the process of following the advice in this book.

ISBNs: 978-1-57023-388-3 (paperback); 978-1-57023-389-0 (eBook)

Library of Congress: 2016934374

Publisher: For information on Impact Publications, including current and forthcoming publications, authors, press kits, online bookstore, newsletters, downloadable catalogs, and submission requirements, visit the left navigation bar on the front page of the main company website: www.impactpublications.com.

Publicity/Rights: For information on publicity, author interviews, and subsidiary rights, contact the Media Relations Department: Tel. 703-361-7300, Fax 703-335-9486, or email: query@impactpublications.com.

Sales/Distribution: All distribution and special sales inquiries should be directed to the publisher: Sales Department, IMPACT PUBLICATIONS, 9104 Manassas Drive, Suite N, Manassas Park, VA 20111-5211, Tel. 703-361-7300, Fax 703-335-9486, or email: query@impactpub lications.com. All bookstore and eBook sales are handled through Impact's trade distributor: National Book Network, 15200 NBN Way, Blue Ridge Summit, PA 17214, Tel. 1-800-462-6420.

Quantity Discounts: We offer quantity discounts on bulk purchases. Please review our discount schedule for this book at www.impactpublications.com or contact the Special Sales Department, Tel. 703-361-0255.

The Authors: Authors of more than 30 books on resumes, cover letters, keywords, hiring, and career management, Wendy Enelow and Louise Kursmark are two of America's leading career professionals who have played major roles in promoting the resume writing and career coaching professions. As certified industry leaders, they are both Master Resume Writers (MRW), Job and Career Transition Coaches (JCTC), Credentialed Career Managers (CCM), and Certified Professional Resume Writers (CPRW). In addition to their regular public speaking and training activities, they are frequently interviewed/quoted by major media, including *The Wall Street Journal, Time Magazine, Chicago Tribune, LA Times, Washington Post, ABC News,* and *Money Magazine.* They can be contacted as follows: wendy@wendyenelow.com and louise@ louisekursmark.com.

Contents

Introduction

KEYWORDS ARE A CRITICAL COMPONENT of *every* job seeker's resume. Whether you are a graduating student, professional, techie, manager, executive, career changer, return-to-work parent, ex-offender, or have moved quickly from one job to the next, your resume *must* be filled with keywords that relate to the jobs, industries, and professions you are targeting.

Why?

Simply put, keywords are the foundation for all online resume scanning systems (more formally known as Applicant Tracking Systems—ATS). Whenever you upload your resume online, respond to a job posting, or email a recruiter, the very first thing that happens in almost all situations is a keyword scan of your resume.

Do you have the right keywords (skills and qualifications) for the position? If yes, your resume will pass the keyword scan and you'll move along in the hiring process. If not, you'll be passed over. It's that straightforward.

FreeDictionary.com defines a "keyword" as:

- A significant or descriptive word.

- A word used as a reference point for other words or information.

When you use the "right" keywords—words that are appropriate to you, your career, your industry and experiences—you convey that you have the specific qualifications employers are looking for. You position yourself as a knowledgeable insider, and you make it easy for employers to understand where you fit into their organization.

In this book we help you identify just what those "right" keywords are *for you* and how to use them—powerfully and appropriately—in all of your career marketing materials. Note that keywords are not just for resumes. They are also essential components for your cover letters, thank-you letters, LinkedIn profile, interviews, and all other job search communications.

To make this book as easy as possible to use, we've structured it so that you can use the parts you need and bypass those that are not relevant to your career. Just follow these simple instructions.

1. Read Chapter 1 to learn about the five principal categories of keywords and how to use them. You'll be surprised at the wide range of keywords and keyword categories—much broader than you might think!

2. Find the chapters that match the industries and professions that you are targeting. Review the top 100 keywords that we show for each, select the ones in which you have experience—whether from work, education, volunteer activities, special projects, or any other area—and incorporate as many as you can into all of your career documents.

3. Review the resumes and cover letters that accompany each chapter to see how the right keywords were integrated throughout each document. These professionally written job search materials will also give you some ideas for how to write, format, and design your own.

4. Read the sample interview questions that we've included as a bonus in each chapter. These short examples will give you insight into how to respond to frequently asked interview questions and integrate keywords into your answers.

5. Be sure to use the reference tools in the Appendix. You'll find our list of 425 resume writing verbs and a list of 221 personality descriptors to showcase critical soft skills (another category of keywords).

In this 2nd edition of *The Best Keywords for Resumes, Cover Letters, and Interviews,* we've also included a special chapter for people with challenging career situations—career changers, people who have been unemployed for long periods of time, moms and dads returning to work, ex-offenders, those with a choppy work history, and others. If you fall into any of these categories, you do face unique obstacles in your job search, so be certain to pay special attention to Chapter 26.

Beyond all of the tactical issues surrounding keywords and online job search is the fact that keywords add tremendous value for human readers. Keywords make your resume and other career messages rich and deep in content, tell a compelling story, and resonate with hiring managers who are seeking qualified candidates with precisely the qualifications (keywords) that you've showcased.

If you can use keywords effectively, you will position yourself above the competition and generate more leads, more interviews, and more opportunities!

Chapter 1

Understanding Keywords

What They Are and Why They Are a Must for Your Job Search

I N THE CONTEXT OF WRITING RESUMES, cover letters, LinkedIn profiles, thank-you letters, personal websites, and all other career communications, keywords are best defined as:

> Words (generally nouns and adjectives) that communicate the specific skills, qualifications, experience, education, professional and technical credentials, and other essential information that supports an individual's job targets and career objectives.

To clarify, not every keyword is just a single word. For example, for many industries and professions the term "customer service" is important, yet it's really a two-word phrase. When we refer to keywords in this book, we are referring to both single keywords and multiple-word keyword phrases.

As you'll read in the following pages, keywords fall into five specific categories, each important in helping your resume get noticed so that you have the opportunity for an interview that can lead to a job offer.

Why Do Keywords Matter?

Keywords are vital for every job seeker, no matter the job or industry. They are a must for everyone—graduating students, professionals, technical personnel, managers, executives, career changers, return-to-work moms and dads, ex-offenders, those with a steady work history and those who have hopped from one job to the next … every single person at any skill level in every profession.

Keywords, once more commonly referred to as buzzwords, are the words that communicate that you have the core skills a company is seeking in a qualified candidate. The use and importance of keywords has surged in reaction to technology changes that have forever altered the processes of job search and candidate selection.

Every time you upload your resume or respond to an online job posting, your resume will immediately pass through an Applicant Tracking System (ATS), where it will be scanned for keywords. The more keyword matches, the more likely your resume will "pass" the scan and move on to the next step—generally a review by a human being who will determine whether or not to move you forward in the hiring process.

Because of ATS and other technological factors that have transformed the employment landscape, the early stages of job search have become a very cut-and-dried process. Either you have the "right" keywords or you don't; either you have as many keyword matches as required for a particular position or you don't.

Your challenge is to be certain that you've included as many keywords as you can—as relevant to your skills, qualifications, experience, educational credentials, and more—so that your resume does pass through ATS and keyword scanning and you do get the opportunity for an interview. If those all-important keywords aren't there, you'll simply be passed over.

Once your resume does reach a human being, keywords are just as important. Employers will evaluate your resume against all others that have passed the automated scan, seeking to determine if you have the right combination of skills and attributes they are seeking. Their judgment can move your resume to the top of the stack or bury it so far down that you never get the chance to interview.

Understanding the concept of keywords, and using all of the right keywords throughout your resume, will give you the very best chance to be selected, interviewed, and ultimately hired.

Five Categories of Keywords

Keywords fall into five distinct categories:

- Hard Skills and Factual Data
- Soft Skills and Attributes
- Employment Details
- Education and Training Credentials
- General Information

We'll explore each of these categories individually.

Hard Skills and Factual Data

Most people think of this category when we talk about keywords. It represents the skills and qualifications associated with a particular industry, profession, or job. For example, keywords for most nursing jobs would include patient care, charting and documentation, emergency response, patient teaching, vitals monitoring … the list is extensive.

Because it represents the core qualifications for a particular job, this category of keywords is the most important. It covers:

- Knowledge, Skills, and Qualifications
- Specific Technology Skills
- Quantified Achievements
- Areas of Expertise
- Industry-Specific Language
- Core Job Functions

Soft Skills and Attributes

Soft skills and attributes are capabilities that an individual possesses that are important on the job but are not necessarily specific to an industry or profession. This list includes:

- Communications
- Organization and Prioritization
- Reliability and Dependability
- Initiative
- Interpersonal Relationships
- Teamwork and Collaboration
- Honesty and Ethics
- Energy and Enthusiasm

Employment Details

Some of the most important keywords used by a recruiter or hiring manager have to do with your past employment experience. Employers are often looking for candidates who have held specific job titles or worked for specific companies, and they use that data as the foundation for their keyword scans. It's easy to see how you can quickly be taken out of consideration if the company is looking only for engineering technicians who've worked at Intel or Samsung.

This category of keywords includes:

- Job Titles
- Product Names
- Customer Names
- Employer Names
- Competitive Company Names
- Length of Employment—in each job and with each company

Education and Training Credentials

Just as with employment details, specific educational and training information can be the essential keywords for a candidate search. Certain companies or hiring managers may look for people with specific degrees from specific universities and will tailor their keyword searches accordingly.

In this category of keywords, you'll find:

- College and University Names
- College Degrees, Majors, and Minors
- Credentials and Licenses
- Internships, Fellowships, and Sabbaticals

- Technical Training and Certifications
- Training Programs and Training Organizations

General Information

Hiring managers and recruiters use a number of other keywords to electronically scan resumes and identify their top candidates. For example, a company that wants to interview only local candidates will use location as a key search term.

General information keywords include:

- Cities, States, Zip Codes, and Countries
- Foreign Languages
- Board Positions

- Professional Affiliations
- Civic and Fraternal Organizations
- Honors and Awards

Where to Put Keywords

In your resume, you have numerous options about how and where to integrate your keywords to create the perception that you're well qualified for your target positions. As you review the following guidelines and examples, bear in mind that you should try to integrate keywords into as many areas as possible, creating keyword-rich content throughout the resume to continually reinforce your qualifications.

Note that in all of the examples below, the keywords are in bold print so that you can easily identify them. When writing your resume, you may choose to bold some of these terms, but be careful that you don't overuse bold print. Too much bold defeats your purpose in trying to draw visual attention to specific information.

Career Summary

The opening section of your resume provides excellent opportunities to showcase your most important keywords. A headline, subheading, and short paragraph or bullet list can be packed full of relevant terms.

Marketing and Business Development Professional
Emerging Technology Products and Service Solutions

Six years' experience helping **high-growth technology** and **telecommunications** companies launch **new products**, gain **market share**, and establish a strong **social media** presence. Specific expertise in **product development, technology commercialization, brand revitalization, and go-to-market strategy.**

Skills List

One of the quickest and easiest ways to enrich your resume with keywords is to create a "key skills" or "core competencies" list (usually a double-column list of keywords) as part of your career summary at the top of your resume.

Signature Skills

- Post-Acquisition Integration
- Multinational Organizational Design
- Business Strategy and Execution
- Team Building, Mentoring and Leadership

- New Venture Launch
- Emerging Market Opportunities
- Resources Delivery and Operations Support
- Strategic Alliances and Business Partnerships

Job Descriptions and Achievement Statements

Use keywords generously when writing about your jobs and achievements. If you are like most job seekers, you'll find this fairly easy to do, because these keywords are the precise terms that describe what you did on the job—assuming that your past positions align with your current objectives.

Advanced from part-time sales position to **Manager** of one of the area's most exclusive women's **retail clothing stores** within less than two years of hire. Direct all aspects of **merchandise acquisition and display, store operations, staffing,** and **customer relationship management.**

- ◆ Averaged 25% annual **revenue growth**. Consistently outpaced and outperformed emerging **market competition** from both **big-box** and **specialty stores.**
- ◆ Built an established **book of business** with hundreds of **repeat customers** across all **demographics.**
- ◆ Expanded beyond **apparel** into **high-end handbags, shoes, jewelry,** and **accessories** to further increase annual **sales** and meet changing **market demand.**
- ◆ **Hired** and **trained** more than 20 personnel over the past 10 years, 14 of whom are still employed with the company. Built and sustained a **collaborative sales team** and working environment.

Education

Intersperse keywords through your education section now that you know keywords can include colleges and degrees, professional credentials, and related factual information.

AAS in Paralegal Litigation (2016) and **BA in Political Science** (2016)
Dual Concentrations: Public Policy and Civil and Women's Rights
Current **GPA—3.83** | **President's Honor Roll** | Member—**Phi Beta Kappa**
VIRGINIA COMMONWEALTH UNIVERSITY, Richmond, VA

AAS in General Studies, Cum Laude (2012)
CENTRAL VIRGINIA COMMUNITY COLLEGE, Lynchburg, VA

Technical Skills Section

If you're in a profession where your specific skills in information technology, tele-communications, digital media, engineering, and related disciplines are primary qualifications, be sure to integrate those details into your resume—either in the summary or in a separate Technology Qualifications or Technology Profile section.

TECHNOLOGY PROFILE

.Net 2, 0, 3, 3.5 … C# … Transact-SQL … Microsoft 2014 SQL Server … SQL Server Integration Services (SSIS) … Windows Server 2008 Clustering … VMWare ESX Server … ASP.net … Neural Networks … Decision Tree Analysis … Clustering Algorithms … Genetic Algorithms … 3PAR Storage Systems

---

Additional Keyword Sections

Integrate other keywords from the five categories above into whatever sections within your resume are most appropriate. Many will fit easily into your summary while others might require separate sections such as Professional Affiliations, Civic Affiliations, Board Positions, Foreign Languages, or Volunteer Experience.

Professional and Leadership Affiliations

◆ **Board Director and Management Committee Member, Economy League of Greater Philadelphia** (2008 to Present)

◆ **Board Director, Executive Committee Member and Fund Development Chair, Maternity Care Coalition** (2005 to 2016)

◆ Member, **Society for Health Care Strategy and Market Development** (1990 to Present)

◆ Member, **Health Care Strategists** (2011 to 2014)

Keywords in Job Search Letters, Interviews, LinkedIn Profiles, and Other Career Communications

Keywords are important in all of your career marketing messages!

When writing **cover letters, thank-you notes, bios,** and other career communications, you can scatter keywords throughout the text—in paragraphs or bulleted lists of items—wherever they most comfortably fit and work well with the text that you're writing. Quite often, these documents are also put through electronic scanning systems, so you want them to be rich with keywords. Just as critically, when people read these documents, you want the right keywords to resonate with them and instantly communicate that you are a qualified candidate.

SPECIAL NOTE ABOUT LETTERS: Just as resumes have changed over the years and become more modern in style, format, and content, so have cover letters. In this book, you'll find samples of both "traditional" cover letters that job seekers and professional resume writers have used for years, along with e-notes—the modern version of the cover letter.

You can upload e-notes in response to job postings, just as with other cover letters. And, when sending your resume via email, use the e-note as the text of your email message, so that readers don't have to click to open your letter. It's right there for them to read.

As you'll notice from the samples, e-notes tend to be shorter in length than cover letters. Both styles of letter should be filled with keywords that will resonate with recruiters, hiring managers, HR professionals, and, of course, electronic keyword scanning systems.

In **interviews,** your use of keywords conveys that you know your job, your industry, and what's important to your interviewer. Keywords are the language of your profession, and interviews give you the opportunity to speak that language fluently with the people who have the power to hire you.

In the following chapters you'll find suggested interview responses—loaded with keywords!—to commonly asked interview questions. These scripts will give you good ideas for incorporating your unique keywords into your own interview messages.

The use of keywords in your **LinkedIn** profile is just as important as in your resume. Hiring managers and recruiters perform keyword searches on LinkedIn, looking for candidates with specific skills and qualifications, just as they scan your resume for keywords. Consider these additional tips when creating your LinkedIn profile.

- LinkedIn gives you many options for how and where to include your key-words—in the summary, job descriptions, education, and various other categories you can add to your profile to showcase the breadth and depth of your qualifications.

- LinkedIn allows you to upload digital and multimedia files—such as PowerPoint or SlideShare presentations, charts, tables, graphs, infographics, and videos—where you can strategically integrate essential keywords to get even more attention. Although keywords from these add-ons might not appear in preliminary keyword searches, they are definitely an added bonus when a person reviews your profile.

- Another powerful benefit of LinkedIn is its generous space allocation. When writing your resume, your goal is to keep it to 1–2 pages in most cases. However, LinkedIn allows 2,000 characters for the summary, 2,000 for each job description, and lots of space for all of the other information. You have an expansive platform to integrate all of your essential keywords.

The Honesty in Keywords

As you've learned in this chapter, integrating keywords into your career documents is critical. Honesty is just as important. Don't claim to have "expertise in" things you've done only a handful of times. Instead, communicate that you have "basic skills" in those job functions.

Conversely, don't undersell yourself either. If you've been managing budgets and financial reporting for 15 years, you can probably feel confident writing about your "expertise in" or "leadership of" those and related job skills. Don't shortchange yourself with words like "experience in" or "participated in." They are not nearly as powerful.

SPEAKING OF POWERFUL … Look at pages 169–173 for our list of 425 verbs to strengthen your resume writing process. No more "responsible for" sentences! Instead, write with verve by using verbs that are clear and strong—coordinate, create, deliver, increase, manage, negotiate, observe, represent, upgrade…. If you write with power, you'll make your resume memorable and distinctive, two key elements in getting noticed and getting hired.

Whether you're creating a double-column keyword list in your summary or incorporating keywords into your job descriptions, be certain to frame those words accurately so readers will understand your specific level of experience in everything you write. Honesty is vital in every area of your job search.

"Cheating" Electronic Keyword Scanning

Now that we've just written all about honesty, we're going to veer off course a bit and address how to handle the situation if you don't have much if any experience related to your job search objectives—and therefore can't naturally use those keywords throughout your resume. When transitioning from one career to another this can often be the case.

First, stop and think carefully about skills that do transition from one industry or one job to another. If you have great computer skills, a wealth of experience in purchasing, numerous years as a classroom teacher, you have acquired skills (keywords) that *will* translate to other industries and professions. Think long and hard about what your transitioning keywords are and showcase them prominently.

In instances where there truly are no keywords that translate from your past experience to your future goals, you may be able to pass an electronic resume scan by using an objective to front-load your resume with keywords. Here are two great examples for someone looking for a position in sales:

OBJECTIVE:

Field Sales position with opportunity to build and strengthen skills in **customer relations, territory management,** and **revenue growth.**

CAREER OBJECTIVE:

Field Sales | Customer Relations | Territory Management | Revenue Growth

In neither of those examples are you stating that you have experience in those functions/keywords. You're simply integrating them into your resume to demonstrate that you know what skills are required for the position—and using them to help you pass the keyword scan.

SPECIAL NOTE TO GRADUATING STUDENTS: Even though you might not have any work experience that is directly related to your job target, you did take many classes (e.g., Economics, Accounting, Financial Analysis and Reporting, Statistics) that are related. Use those as your primary keywords to pass the keyword scan. And, don't worry … if a company is seeking to hire a graduating student, chances are they don't expect you to have much, if any, experience.

Where to Find Keywords

The best place to find keywords is this book. Look for the chapters that are most relevant to your job targets, review the keyword lists, and select the ones that accurately reflect your skills, experience, education, and other qualifications. Integrate those keywords into your resume, cover letters, interviews, and all other job search communications.

Other valuable resources for identifying critical keywords include:

- Online job postings
- Job descriptions
- Company websites (job postings, "About Us," "Mission")
- LinkedIn groups (job postings, conversations) and LinkedIn company pages
- Social media engagement
- Professional associations (newsletters, meetings, conferences, networking)
- Books, trade journals, and industry dictionaries

Mine these resources to identify other keywords that are relevant to you, your job history, and your current career objectives.

One Final Keyword Note

In this chapter, we've focused on what keywords are and how to use them in your resume and other career messages. You can use those same keywords as the foundation for your online job search—the terms you'll use to identify job opportunities. Type in a keyword and all the positions that have that term will be included in your search results.

Keywords serve double duty as both the important searchable words in your resume *and* the search terms you'll use to find the right positions!

How to Use This Book

Step #1: Find Your Keywords

Locate the chapters that match the industries and professions that you are targeting. Review the top 100 keywords that we share for each, select the ones in which you have experience—whether from work, education, volunteer activities, special projects, or any other area—and incorporate as many as you can into all of your career materials. These are your hard skills keywords that are the most important.

Step #2: Review Resume and Letter Samples

Each chapter includes a sample resume and cover letter integrating appropriate keywords. Note that the resume and letter are for *different* job seekers because we wanted to showcase the broadest possible sets of keywords. You'll find some of these keywords in the top 100 lists at the beginning of each chapter, while others will be keywords that are specific to that individual and his or her job search. Use these samples as inspiration for the content, format, and design of your own resume and letter(s).

Step #3: Read Sample Interview Questions

The sample interview questions that we've included will give you insight into how to integrate your keywords into some of the most frequently asked interview questions. You'll notice how keywords are used both *generally* and *specifically* to describe knowledge, expertise, experience, and unique accomplishments. Again, as with the resume and letter samples, some of these terms will appear in the keyword lists at the beginning of each chapter while others will be specific to that individual job seeker.

Step #4: Pay Special Attention to the "Challenging Job Search" Chapter

If you're facing unique challenges in your job search—military career transition, returning to work after a lengthy absence, returning to work after incarceration, a history of job hopping, or any one of a number of other unique job search challenges, pay special attention to the "Challenging Job Search" Chapter and the accompanying resumes. These resources will help you best understand how to integrate your vital keywords no matter your challenge or situation.

Step #5: Use the Verb List and Personality Descriptors

In the Appendix, you'll find a list of 425 resume writing verbs to help you write with power, along with a list of 221 personality descriptors to showcase your most important soft skills.

Chapter 2

Accounting and Auditing

Top 100 Keywords

Account Analysis &
   Reconciliation

Accounting

Accounts Payable

Accounts Receivable

Analysis

Asset Allocation

Asset Management

Asset Purchase

Audit Controls

Audit Management

Audit Review Procedures

Auditing

Balance Sheet

Bank Reconciliation

Banking

Billing

Bookkeeping

Budget

Budget Forecasting

Business Administration

Business Statistics

Capital Budget

Cash Accounting

Cash Management

Cash Receipts

Collections

Commercial Banking

Computer Systems

Contract Administration

Corporate Banking

Corporate Tax

Cost Accounting

Cost Reduction

Cost Savings

Cost-Benefit Analysis

Credit & Collections

Credit Management

Credit Terms & Conditions

Data Collection & Analysis

Earnings

Economics

Efficiency Improvement

Equity Analysis

Excel

Expense Accounting

External Audits

Financial Accounting

Financial Analysis & Reporting

Financial Audits

Financial Controls

Financial Modeling

Financial Ratios

Financial Statements

Forecasting

Forensic Accounting

Funds Accounting

General Ledger

Generally Accepted Accounting Principles (GAAP)

Income Statement

Information Systems

Information Technology

Internal Audits

Internal Controls

Inventory Audit

Invoices

Job Costing

Journals

Ledgers

Letters of Credit

Line of Credit

Management Accounting

Notes Payable

Notes Receivable

Operating Budget

Operating Expenses

Operating Income

Operational Audits

Partnership Accounting

Policies & Procedures

Profit & Loss (P&L) Analysis

Profitability Analysis

Project Accounting

Public Accounting

Receivables

Regulatory Compliance & Reporting

Regulatory Standards

Return on Assets (ROA)

Return on Equity (ROE)

Return on Investment (ROI)

Risk Management

Sarbanes-Oxley (SOX) Compliance

Spreadsheets

Staff Accounting

Statistical Analysis & Reporting

Statistical Modeling

Stockholder Reporting

Technology

Trust Accounting

Variance Analysis

Workpapers

TERRY OLSEN

612-788-9999   Minneapolis, MN 55418   terry.olsen@comcast.net

ACCOUNTANT

Five years' experience in all phases of general accounting, financial planning, and financial reporting. Excellent analytical skills and ability to communicate complex financial data in easy-to-understand terms.

PROFESSIONAL EXPERIENCE

ACCOUNTANT, 2013–Present
O'Connor & Hannan, L.L.P., Minneapolis, MN

Perform a wide range of accounting and finance functions at the headquarters office of a national law firm.

Financial Planning, Analysis & Reporting

- Created, interpreted, and reported financial information in support of general business operations and long-term strategic planning functions.
- Prepared and presented monthly financial information package to senior management team.
- Developed financial forecasts, projections, and analytical tools.
- Compiled financial data for sensitive corporate, legal, credit, and general business issues.

General Accounting

- Coordinated month-end closings, prepared monthly analyses of all balance sheet accounts, and facilitated preparation of annual financial statements.
- Managed all A/P and A/R functions for completion of month-end financial statements.
- Reconciled revenue accounts to general ledger and subsidiary reports.
- Streamlined and enhanced accounting, reporting, and analysis techniques.

Budgeting & Cash Management

- Prepared and managed annual budgets for operations, overhead expenditures, and miscellaneous costs. Administered up to $10M in annual funds.
- Recommended and implemented improved variance analysis and expense forecasting methods.
- Formulated cash projections, monitored cash flow, and implemented cash controls.

Information Technology

- Actively involved in the planning and implementation of automation and upgrade projects for accounting and financial systems.
- Trained users in all areas of the company on new systems and technologies.

ACCOUNTS RECEIVABLE ADMINISTRATOR, 2011–2013
Norstrom Associates, St. Paul, MN

Managed the accounts receivable function for a large management consulting firm. Coordinated billing, credit, collections, inventory, and reporting functions. Prepared monthly sales and cash receipt reports, account analyses, journal entries, customer credit adjustments, and bad debt write-offs.

EDUCATION

B.A., ACCOUNTING & POLITICAL SCIENCE, 2011
University of Minnesota

Marcella J. Koenig

908-345-1110 • marcellakoenig@gmail.com
LinkedIn.com/in/MarcellaKoenig

March 5, 2016

Steven del Prisco
VP Finance
Pandex, Inc.
457 White River Parkway
Jersey City, NJ 07306

Dear Mr. del Prisco:

James Wishlow—a fellow member of the New Jersey Chapter, Institute of Internal Auditors—told me that you have an opening for an experienced auditor, and he strongly suggested that I throw my hat in the ring!

My professional experiences and successes will be of value to Pandex, with its diverse lines of business and global operations. Highlights include:

- Progressive career as member of the audit staff for 3 Fortune 500 companies, each in vastly differing industries and customer markets, and each operating internationally.

- Consistent record of improving audit strategies, processes, controls, and technologies.

- Success in positioning audit as a business partner, not an adversary, with both internal and external audiences.

I work well in high-pressure and demanding positions and am known for meeting "impossible" deadlines without compromising quality or accuracy. Most importantly, I am passionate about the importance of the audit function and its value to corporate operations and the bottom line.

James has told me many good things about the culture at Pandex and the excellent working relationships between departments. That is precisely the environment where I do my best work, and I am quite excited to explore this opportunity further. To that end, I will call your office next week to schedule a meeting.

Thank you.

Sincerely,

Marcella J. Koenig

Keyword Answers to Interview Questions

Tell me about yourself.

I'm an accounting associate who has worked for both public and private companies in the Charlotte metro area. With each of my four employers, I've moved quickly through increasingly responsible accounting and financial support positions. In fact, with Farmer and Associates, my current employer, I was promoted within three months of hire and again just six months later.

I've always loved numbers and did very well in all of my accounting and related courses in both high school and college. If offered the opportunity to take an "easy" English class or a high-level accounting course, I always chose accounting! It's how I'm programmed, so to speak, and what I am destined to do in my career.

What is the most valuable skill you bring to our company?

My two greatest skills are accuracy and precision. It's never good enough to reconcile to within a hundred dollars or even a single dollar. It must reconcile to the penny—whether a petty cash account or a million-dollar credit line.

As a result of what most consider a good compulsion, I've taken the liberty of developing a set of procedures for others to use in their reconciliation activities. We've expanded it from headquarters to all 32 of our locations in the US and, as a result, have strengthened our overall reporting and reconciliation capabilities. Even more importantly, we just passed an external audit with zero exceptions for the first time in the company's history.

What is your most significant achievement?

Since I've already addressed my successes in account reconciliation, I'll share my contributions to the implementation of an entire suite of JD Edwards software solutions. When I arrived at Farmer, we were using antiquated technology for several years. Rather than transition slowly, we undertook a massive transformation of the entire technology system for accounting and finance.

My efforts in documenting our accounting requirements, testing software solutions, and working with the JD Edwards team on the implementation were notable, and I was credited with helping achieve full implementation well ahead of schedule. With a goal of six months for the project, we were up and running at 100% in less than four months. It was a great success for me and my teammates.

Chapter 3

Business Administration and Office Management

Top 100 Keywords

Account Management

Accounting

Administration

Administrative Affairs

Administrative Management

Administrative Processes

Administrative Systems

Auditing

Back Office Operations

Banking

Billing

Budgeting

Business Administration

Business Correspondence

Business Travel

Cash Management

Clerical

Client Communications

Client Relationship Management

Committees

Compliance

Computer Networks

Computer Systems

Computer Technology

Confidential Correspondence

Contract Administration

Contracts

Corporate Communications

Corporate Recordkeeping

Corporate Secretary

Customer Communication

Customer Service

Customer Support

Data Collection & Analysis

Data Entry

Database Management

Decision Making

Detail

Digital Technology

Document Management

Documentation

Efficiency Improvement

Electronic Files

Executive Business

Executive Officer Support

Facilities Management

Facilities Renovation

Files Management

Finance Administration

Financial Reporting

Front Office Operations

Government Relations

Human Resources

Leasing

Liaison Affairs

Mail & Messenger Services

Manufacturing Administration

Marketing Administration

Media Relations

Meeting Planning

MS Office Suite – Word, PowerPoint, Excel, Outlook

Multi-Tasking

Networking

Office Administration

Office Equipment

Office Management

Office Relocation

Office Services

Operations Administration

Operations Support

Order Processing

Policies & Procedures

Prioritization

Problem Solving

Process Design

Product Support

Productivity Improvement

Project Administration

Project Management

Proposals

Purchasing

Reception Services

Recordkeeping

Records Management

Regulatory Affairs

Reporting

Resource Management

Sales Administration

Social Media

Special Events

Special Projects

Staff Training & Development

Staffing

Technical Support

Technology

Telecommunications

Time Management

Transportation Administration

Workflow Planning

Workload Demand

ROXANNE WILLIAMS

Washington, DC • 202-695-4208
roxannewilliams@gmail.com
www.LinkedIn.com/in/roxannewilliams

ADMINISTRATIVE MANAGER

Supporting Multi-Site Regional Sales, Marketing, Sales Training & Customer Operations For 15+ Years

Core Competencies:

- Sales & Marketing Support
- Senior Staff Relations & Communications
- Vendor & Customer Communications
- Policy & Procedure Compliance
- Productivity & Performance Management

- Project Planning & Management
- Special Events & Meetings Management
- Problem Solving & Decision Making
- Workload Planning & Prioritization
- Staff Training & Development

PROFESSIONAL EXPERIENCE

RAYBURN MICROSYSTEMS, INC., Washington, DC   2008 to Present

Area Administrative Supervisor

Promoted through a series of increasingly responsible administrative positions supporting large-scale regional sales and customer management programs. Currently work in cooperation with Area Vice President and other senior management to plan and direct administrative affairs for the Southern Area (12 states, 125 field sales reps). Lead a team of 12–15 field administrators. Work independently with little or no direct supervision.

Process Design & Performance Improvement

- Design and implement enhanced administrative processes, procedures, and systems to support rapid regional growth ($450M in 2012 to $830M projected for 2016). Anticipate organizational needs and initiate appropriate actions to obtain resources, technologies, and personnel to meet peak workload demands.

Operating Support

- Consult with Vice President, HR Director, Controller, and other senior staff to plan workload, allocate personnel, coordinate special projects, and facilitate the entire administrative function. Collaborate with management teams to resolve problems impacting efficiency and productivity.

Management Support

- Independently direct administrative affairs on behalf of Vice President. Draft correspondence and other communications, coordinate meetings and calendar requests, prioritize incoming projects, process travel arrangements, and prepare expense reports. Represent Vice President to other departments and divisions.

Special Events Management

- Plan, staff, budget, and manage sales meetings, conferences, leadership programs, and special events. Coordinate communications with hotels, caterers, transportation companies, meeting planners, exhibitors, suppliers, and speakers. Most notable event: 2015 Southern Area Kick-Off Meeting with 300+ attendees.

Human Resources Affairs

- Hire, train, schedule, supervise, and evaluate the work performance of administrative, clerical, and support personnel. Define long-term staffing requirements, coordinate staff training and development programs, and initiate disciplinary action as appropriate. Participate in annual performance reviews and long-range career planning.

Facilities Management

- Coordinate office relocations, consolidations, and renovation projects to accommodate growth and new hires. Redesign existing space layouts to enhance efficiency and ensure optimum utilization of all physical resources. Manage telecommunications, security, and other systems installations. Saved $6300 on proposed $7000 fire systems upgrade project through strategic negotiations and vendor management.

Purchasing Management

- Plan and direct purchasing programs for office equipment, services, supplies, and furnishings. Source new vendors, negotiate pricing and discounts, coordinate logistics, and maintain inventory levels. Currently manage purchasing operations through corporate headquarters.

Financial Affairs

- Maintain $50,000 checking account, reconcile petty cash accounts, and prepare informal financial statements for review by senior management. Justify increased spending to meet operating, staffing, facilities, and administrative requirements.

RRT DEVELOPMENT CORPORATION, Alexandria, VA   1999–2008

Executive Assistant to Vice President, Federal Sales Systems Group

Fast-track promotion from Receptionist to Order Operations Clerk to Administrative Assistant to Executive Assistant. Managed all administrative support functions for a 200-person field sales organization. Trained and supervised less experienced administrative staff.

- Participated in a series of internal change and process redesign initiatives to improve the efficiency of order processing, data entry, proposal preparation, sales administration, and customer service/support.

EDUCATION & CAREER TRAINING

- Frontline Leadership
- Business As Usual Seminar
- Career Architect Planning
- Managing Field Compensation
- Sexual Harassment & Performance Management
- Time Management & Conflict Management

To: CarlaNorris@RecruitingSpecialists.com
From: Michael Rodriguez
Re: Administrative Assistant—Finance/Insurance/Compliance

Ms. Norris—

As a highly qualified Administrative Professional, I offer your client:

- Nine years' experience in progressively challenging administrative roles, culminating as Senior Administrative Associate in Fargo Mutual's compliance division.

- History of initiative and leadership in identifying and eliminating obstacles to productivity.

- Strong skills in tracking, monitoring, documenting, and reporting—I have been referred to as "the vault" for my ability to store and retrieve extensive information securely and efficiently.

- Ability to manage multiple detailed projects simultaneously.

A recent downsizing at Fargo Mutual has eliminated my position. As evidence of the value of my work there, my role will be assumed by the Compliance Director, who has commended me for my professionalism and "get-the-job-done" attitude.

I would like to meet with you to discuss the value I bring to your client's company Thank you.

Sincerely,

Michael Rodriguez
701-300-2379
rodriguez.michael.t@gmail.com
linkedin.com/in/michaeltrodriguez

Keyword Answers to Interview Questions

Tell me about yourself.

Let me begin by sharing that I have more than eight years' experience in office administration with two very interesting organizations—a large mining and construction company and a small, privately owned real estate investment firm.

In both positions, I managed a diverse portfolio of administrative affairs for each company's top executives. I handled business correspondence, contracts, confidential recordkeeping, meeting planning, customer service, and daily business management functions. I'm great with multi-tasking and have enjoyed the rapid pace at each company where I've worked.

Just as important are my very strong skills in technology and social media. I'm an expert in Microsoft Word, Office, and PowerPoint; led a full-scale network upgrade; set up and currently manage our company's LinkedIn, Facebook, and Google pages.

I'm very interested to learn about your current administrative management challenges and how I can be of value to you.

What is the most valuable skill you bring to our company?

What I do best is plan, organize, and execute. No matter the work assignment, special project, or tight time and financial constraints, I have delivered on time, exceeded company goals, and earned a reputation for my ability to get things done—fast and efficiently.

Just as important is my strong work ethic and commitment to both my employer and myself to do the very best that I can to strengthen an organization's administrative structure, systems, and processes. I firmly believe that this is one of the reasons for my rapid promotion with my current employer.

What is your most significant achievement?

In my current position, I was asked to take over responsibility for financial reporting functions that had fallen behind schedule and were not meeting regulatory standards.

Working in partnership with two business management associates, I created a new portfolio of Excel spreadsheets for data collection and analysis. We instituted new accounting and reporting systems and brought the company up to date in less than 60 days. In addition, we introduced a number of new technologies that instantly improved the productivity, efficiency, and quality of the entire financial organization.

Chapter 4

Association and Non-Profit Management

Top 100 Keywords

Administration	Development
Advocacy	Digital Technology
Affiliate Membership	Donor Relations
Association	Economics
Association Management	Education Foundation
Awareness	Educational Programs
Board Relations	Endowment Funds
Board Reporting	Finance
Budget Allocation & Oversight	Financial Management
Budget Reporting	Financial Reporting
Budgeting	Foundation
Chapter	Funding
Communications	Fundraising
Community Outreach	Government Relations
Computer Networks	Government Reporting
Computer Systems	Grant Administration
Computer Technology	Grant Writing
Conferences & Conventions	Grassroots Campaign
Corporate Development	Human Resources
Corporate Giving	Human Rights
Corporate Sponsorship	Humanitarian Relief

In-Kind Funding

Industry Association

Industry Relations

Institutional Affairs

International

Investment Management

Leadership Training &
  Development

Legislative Affairs

Lending

Lobbying

Marketing

Marketing Communications

Media Relations

Member Communications

Member Development

Member Retention

Member Services

Micro-Lending

Mission Planning

Monetary Funding

Multimedia

Networking

Non-Governmental
  Organization (NGO)

Non-Profit

Not-For-Profit

Organization(al) Leadership

Organization(al) Mission

Organization(al) Needs
  Assessment

Organization(al) Vision

Outreach Programs

Partnerships

Policy Development

Political Action Committee (PAC)

Political Affairs

Press Relations

Private Partnerships

Program Funding

Project Management

Public Affairs

Public Partnerships

Public Policy Development

Public Relations

Regulatory Affairs

Regulatory Reporting

Relief Programs

Reporting

Research Foundation

Service Programs

Social Media

Speakers Bureau

Special Events

Sponsorship

Strategic Planning

Sustainability

Technology

Telecommunications

Volunteer Recruitment

Volunteer Training

Bianca Garza

Chevy Chase, MD 22351

410-669-4352 ▪ bianca.garza@gmail.com

NOT-FOR-PROFIT ASSOCIATION EXECUTIVE

Dynamic 10-year management career leading large-scale, not-for-profit organizations. Expert in evaluating organizational needs and creating proactive development, relief, service, and outreach programs that have consistently achieved/surpassed operating goals.

Extensive international experience with excellent knowledge of the political and social cultures, trends, and operating environments in Africa, Latin America, and Europe.

Fluent Spanish and French.

Core Competencies
- Development Issues—Theory & Practice
- Fundraising & Marketing
- Multi-Site Management
- Strategic Planning & Policy Development
- Humanitarian Relief
- Public & Private Partnerships
- Board Relations & Donor Negotiations
- Health Care & Education Services

PROFESSIONAL EXPERIENCE

HUMAN RELIEF SERVICES—HRS, Landover, MD   **1998 to Present**

Progressed through leadership roles with one of world's largest and most diversified private volunteer organizations that sponsors sustainable self-help programs in areas of agriculture, primary health care, education, micro-credit lending, and human rights. HRS is also one of the world's leaders in emergency relief assistance.

Throughout majority of tenure, served as Senior Manager of regional operations worldwide with full responsibility for strategic planning, programming, financial management, human resources, administration, marketing, resource acquisition, and daily operations management. Demonstrated expertise in fundraising, cross-cultural relations, team building, and leadership.

Special Assistant to the Deputy Executive Director—World Headquarters (2015 to Present)

Promoted to newly created position and challenged to expand international programming by leveraging resources from affiliate European organizations.

- Conceived idea and currently directing development of an innovative international support program combining monetary and in-kind fundraising in cooperation with farmers and local governments.

- Secured $15M in new funding from Eurozone nations to support program development and launch.

Coordinator—Domestic Outreach & Education—World Headquarters (2012 to 2015)

Created new strategy to expand cooperative efforts with the organization's 196 affiliates nationwide.

- Launched a portfolio of marketing, educational, and communication programs to expand awareness, strengthen partnerships, and increase program funding.

- Held collateral responsibility for numerous annual special events and fundraising initiatives to support worldwide operations.

- Planned strategies and directed efforts that raised $14M in funding.

Bianca Garza

Page 2
410-669-4352 ▪ bianca.garza@gmail.com

HRS—*continued*

Regional Director—Central America & Caribbean, Nicaragua (2009 to 2012)

Directed HRS operations in 6 countries and large-scale special projects in 3 other nations. Allocated more than $25M in annual funds to expand agricultural, primary health care, sanitation, micro-credit lending, and other cutting-edge development programs in highly charged political environment.

- Transitioned program "ownership" to local nationals by introducing quality-driven program management processes, audit review standards, and project management/review protocols.

- Structured, negotiated, and obtained $1.3M grant from USAID to improve water and sanitation services.

Regional Director—East Africa & the Indian Ocean, Kenya (2006 to 2009)
Deputy Director—Africa Region / Director—African Development Group (2003 to 2006)

Spearheaded $20M initiative to refocus African development strategy. Designed and piloted new initiative emphasizing program ownership, popular participation, and institution building and was subsequently promoted to implement across 9-country East Africa/Indian Ocean region. Managed $80M–$100M in annual funding and 250+ paid staff.

- Led the largest and most sophisticated program in the 53-year history of the organization, delivering relief services to 2.6 million displaced Ethiopians each month.

- Spearheaded development of the first-ever cross-border relief programs in Somalia.

- Restructured management hierarchy throughout the 9-country region, implemented decentralized management system, and created a local ownership philosophy to strengthen program commitment of both HRS and local national teams.

- Created model for worldwide implementation over the next 10 years.

Program Director (1999 to 2003) with assignments in Southern Africa, East Africa, and Central America.

Program Assistant (1998 to 1999) in Guatemala, Nicaragua, and Ecuador.

EDUCATION

MBA—Finance/International Business, Columbia University Graduate School of Business
BS—Economics, Boston College

DAVID McANDREWS
617-469-3826 • david.mcandrews@yahoo.com • Boston, MA 02210
www.LinkedIn.com/in/DavidMcAndrews

March 5, 2016

John D. Valenti, Chairman of the Board
International Association of Painters
2938 Main Street
Charlestown, MA 02127

Dear Mr. Valenti:

Re: Vice President Operations—IAP

As one of the top 3 executives in a national nonprofit in the real estate industry, I played a leading role in building NARP from an unknown entity into a nationally recognized organization with efficient operations, high member satisfaction, and a strong bottom line. My contributions can best be summarized in 4 areas:

Financial Leadership

I built NARP's entire financial, accounting, internal auditing, and budgeting infrastructure from the ground floor. This included developing a progressive cash management program, managing payroll and related tax affairs, negotiating lines of credit, and handling investments valued in excess of $3M. Further, I launched a series of aggressive cost-saving initiatives that reduced overhead as much as 40% and enabled us to boost our investment reserve 60%.

Human Resources Leadership

When I joined NARP there was no HR function. Under my leadership, we developed recruitment and benefit programs, retirement plans, training seminars, job descriptions, employee manuals, and more—creating a fully integrated HR organization able to support the association as it continued to grow.

Office Technology

To keep pace with rapid changes in technology and enhance organizational productivity, I spearheaded the acquisition and implementation of a host of computer systems designed specifically for association management. Further, I led the acquisition of several generations of telecommunication systems.

Program & Convention Management

My contributions to programming, conventions, and meetings has focused on planning and logistics. I have coordinated efforts for up to 10 events per year, hosting some 20,000 total participants. In addition, I have been active in providing content development concepts to better service our national membership.

Now that NARP has been absorbed into New York-based IREA, I am seeking a new opportunity in association management, ideally with an organization such as IAP that would value my deep knowledge of the real estate industry and the business and nonprofit climate in the Boston area. Your current opening for a VP Operations seems an excellent fit, and I would welcome the opportunity to discuss it with you.

Sincerely,

David McAndrews

Keyword Answers to Interview Questions

Tell me about yourself.

Since beginning my career in association management 12 years ago, I've had a great run! Starting as a membership development associate, I earned 6 promotions, each time retaining all of my previous responsibilities while taking on the challenges of each new assignment.

As such, I have a wealth of experience in all facets of association operations—budgeting, educational programming, member services, public relations, media affairs, board relations, policy development, and regulatory affairs.

Whether designing a marketing campaign, planning special events, negotiating with industry trade groups, or establishing a new member program, I've done it all and done it well—as evidenced by the results: growth in membership, growth in sponsorships, growth in conference and meeting attendance, increases in media mentions, and more. I'm interested in learning how I might be able to do the same for you.

What is the most valuable skill you bring to our company?

Undoubtedly, my greatest skill and value to any organization is my ability to build camaraderie across diverse interest groups. This is best exemplified by a recent environmental project requiring the full cooperation of our association, both state and federal regulatory agencies, local politicians, our membership, and the general public.

Each group had its own entirely different agenda, and these differences had put the project in a very tenuous situation. By opening channels of communication, we were able to identify the core issues impeding the project's progress, and I was able to facilitate their prompt and efficient resolution. The project was brought to closure, achieving everyone's goals and meeting our association's objectives.

What is your most significant achievement?

My greatest achievement has been my success in membership development and retention. When I joined my current employer, our membership was stagnant and retention was a constant problem.

Today, our membership is increasing an average of 22% annually and our retention rates are the highest they've ever been. In fact, my team and I are currently consulting with a sister organization to share our insights into member services and member outreach.

Chapter 5

Banking

Top 100 Keywords

Acquisitions

Asset-Based Lending

Asset Management

Asset Valuation

Audit Examination

Auditing

Automated Teller Machine (ATM)

Bank Administration

Bank Management

Banking Operations

Banking Regulations

Bankruptcy

Bonds

Borrowers

Branch Operations

Cash Management

Cash Reconciliation

Chapter 7 Bankruptcy

Chapter 11 Bankruptcy

Checking Account

Collections

Commercial Banking

Commercial Credit

Consumer Banking

Consumer Credit

Consumer Lending

Corporate Banking

Corporate Lending

Correspondent Banking

Credit

Credit Cards

Credit Line

Credit Rating

Credit Union

Customer Service

de novo Banking

Debt Financing

Deposit

Depository Services

Electronic Banking

Equity Financing

Fee Income

Foreign Exchange (FX)

Fraud

Global Banking

Home Equity Loan

Income

Interest

Investment Banking

Investor Relations

Leasing

Legal Compliance

Lending

Letter of Credit

Liability Management

Line of Credit

Loan Administration

Loan Processing

Loan Recovery

Loan Underwriting

Lockbox Processing

Merchant Banking

Mergers

Money Market

Mortgage Lending

Mutual Funds

Non-Performing Assets

Portfolio Management

Private Banking

Private Equity

Real Estate Lending

Receivership

Refinancing

Regulatory Compliance

Regulatory Reporting

Relationship Management

Retail Banking

Retail Lending

Return-On-Assets (ROA)

Return-On-Equity (ROE)

Return-On-Investment (ROI)

Risk Management

Savings Account

Savings & Loan

Secondary Markets

Secure Networks & Systems

Secured Lending

Securities

Securities & Exchange
   Commission (SEC)

Stocks

Strategic Planning

Tax Shelter

Technology

Teller Operations

Transaction Banking

Trust Services

Unsecured Lending

Valuation

Wholesale Banking

Workout

CHRISTOPHER CHASE

358-208-9256 ~ ChrisChase@gmail.com ~ LinkedIn.com/in/ChristopherChase

COMMUNITY BANKING EXECUTIVE

Leading Banking Institutions Through Start-up, Turnaround, Merger, Acquisition & Growth

**Delivered strong and sustainable gains in revenue, fee income, and asset value
within highly competitive and volatile markets.**

*Strategic Planning ~ Banking Services & Products ~ Sales & Marketing ~ Deposit Growth
Commercial & Consumer Lending ~ Mortgage Lending ~ Credit Administration ~ Workout & Recovery
IT ~ Finance & Budgeting ~ Human Resources ~ Multi-Site Operations Management*

PROFESSIONAL EXPERIENCE

President & CEO—FINANCIAL FEDERAL   2011–2016

Appointed President & CEO following the merger of Myers Bank, State Bank, and Tress Federal to create Financial Federal. Challenged to lead the new organization through an aggressive reorganization, turnaround, and return to profitability.

Held P&L responsibility for the institution and all business units—Lending, Mortgage Banking, Funds Acquisition, Sales and Marketing, HR, IT, Operations, Finance and Budgeting, Strategic Planning, and Customer Service.

> ➢ Met or exceeded all turnaround objectives for **$750M** savings and loan institution. Consolidated 660 employees in 59 locations in 7 states, to 420 employees in 23 locations throughout Missouri. Transformed 2011 loss of **$21M** to 2015 earnings of **$8M+**.

> ➢ Orchestrated the workout and recovery of more than **$60M** in non-performing assets.

> ➢ Created, launched, and marketed a series of consumer, mortgage, and small commercial lending programs to reestablish the institution and rebuild solvent portfolio.

> ➢ Repositioned new institution within the marketplace, restored confidence within the consumer and commercial communities, and launched a well-targeted marketing and public relations campaign to rebuild market image.

> **NOTE:**   *Appointed Co-Director to facilitate 2-year transition and integration of operations following Prairie Bancorp's acquisition of Financial Federal in 2014.*

Vice President of Administration—MYERS BANK   2005–2011

Member of 5-person executive management team leading the transition of Federal Savings & Loan into a publicly owned federal savings bank (Myers). Redesigned organizational infrastructure, reengineered operations, and guided the institution through a period of rapid growth and diversification. Led strategic planning and market repositioning.

Directed the Administration Division (IT, Human Resources, General Services) with 30 employees and a $5M annual budget. Created dynamic business processes, operations, policies, and procedures to meet changing organizational needs.

> ➢ Recreated Federal through an aggressive M&A program with 6 other institutions to create Myers Bank.

> ➢ Instrumental in building assets from **$140M** to **$680M**, expanding locations from 7 to 47, and increasing employee base from 100 to 500.

CHRISTOPHER CHASE   PAGE 2

358-208-9256 ~ ChrisChase@gmail.com ~ LinkedIn.com/in/ChristopherChase

---

Vice President of Management Systems—FEDERAL SAVINGS & LOAN   2000–2005

Promoted from Management Systems Specialist to VP within 2 years. Evaluated organizational needs and drove the design and implementation of improved operating and administrative processes that impacted all key business units.

Concurrently, spearheaded a number of new programs and services to diversify the bank's portfolio.

- ➢ Invested more than **$2M** in technology upgrades to automate and strengthen operating processes.
- ➢ Orchestrated development, staffing, budgeting, and start-up of property management company to expand statewide real estate practice.
- ➢ Introduced new cash management program, space management systems, security training program, and a portfolio of other internal processes.
- ➢ Directed construction of 4 retail deposit facilities. Brought project in on time and within budget despite construction overrides and accelerating costs.

Director of Claims Processing—MISSOURI WORKER'S COMPANY   1997–2000

Member of 5-person management team challenged to reengineer and modernize the operations, processes, and technologies of $54M fund (80,000+ claims annually).

Led implementation of automated claims processing technology, redesigned core business systems, developed training programs, and supervised 100+ personnel through 7 direct management reports.

Business & Technology Consultant—CMB, INC.   1994–1997

Teaching / Research Assistant—NATIONAL SCIENCE FOUNDATION   1992–1994

EDUCATION

MISSOURI STATE UNIVERSITY

MS Industrial Engineering, 1994
BS Industrial Engineering, 1992

To: **Allison Hentges**
From: **Patricia Jones**
Re: Retail Banking Manager

Dear Ms. Hentges:

With regard to your current opening for a Manager for your South Portland office …

- **If your goal is to increase lending volume,** I originated more than $1 million in mortgages in less than two years.

- **If your goal is to increase deposit growth,** I captured $8.8 million in net deposits in 2015.

- **If your goal is to strengthen your market position and customer image,** I led marketing, business development, and outreach efforts that enabled us to dominate our local market and outperform the competition.

- **If your goal is to enhance customer service,** I spearheaded a number of programs that not only increased customer satisfaction, but improved our staff's focus on service, retention, and performance.

As an experienced Retail Banking Manager with a 10-year record of results, I have the expertise you need and the drive, creativity, and leadership skills to elevate South Portland to the top of your branch network. May we schedule a call to discuss? Thank you.

Patricia Jones
****

801-345-1267
patricia.jones@email.com
LinkedIn Profile: http://www.linkedin.com/in/patriciajones

Keyword Answers to Interview Questions

Tell me about yourself.

Banking is in my blood! My father and two of my uncles were bankers, both of my grandfathers, and three of my brothers. It's the "family business," so to speak.

With that said, let me tell you that I have 12 years' experience in banking, mostly concentrated in commercial lending and commercial credit operations. Although I have done some retail banking, my primary functions have involved structuring and negotiating high-dollar credit transactions for Fortune 500 corporate clients.

In addition, I have a great deal of experience in loan packaging and syndication, equity and debt financing, real estate investment trusts, and loan workout and recovery. In total, I've participated in more than $2.8 billion in transactions over the past five years.

What is the most valuable skill you bring to our company?

My negotiating skills are by far my greatest talent. When others have thought that deals would be impossible to close, I've been able to align all of the partners, negotiate the contracts, and close the transactions.

When terms of specific contracts were unacceptable, I've been able to successfully renegotiate despite conflicting interests. And, when managing debt recovery projects, I've been able to hammer out realistic workouts in often poor economic conditions.

One good example of my negotiating skill is the deal that I struck for Major Foods when we were entering a new market in Eastern Europe. Our goal was to launch a distribution network without an outlay of cash—in essence, we were asking our retail partners to finance the startup for us. I used my negotiating skill to keep everyone at the table, working out terms that were fair and acceptable to all.

What is your most significant achievement?

Last December, I was asked to evaluate a loan package for one of the nation's largest telecommunication companies. Despite the company's strong financial position and overall positive market indicators, the volatility within the technology market concerned me.

As such, despite initial loan committee approval, I was able to demonstrate the potential risks of the transaction to the senior members of the Board of Directors and we withdrew our bank from consideration. Today, that company is bankrupt.

Chapter 6

Construction

Top 100 Keywords

Appraisal

Appreciation

Architectural Drawing

Architectural Rendering

Architecture

Asset Disposition

Asset Management

Asset Valuation

Asset Workout & Recovery

Bid Preparation

Blueprint

Boundary Map

Budgeting

Building Codes

Building Engineering

Building Inspection

Building Standards

Building Trades

Capital Improvement

Civil Engineering

Claims Administration

Code Compliance

Commercial Development

Competitive Bidding

Computer-Aided Design (CAD)

Construction

Construction Crew

Construction Drawings

Construction Engineering

Construction Financing

Construction Management

Construction Site Management

Construction Technology

Construction Trades

Contract Administration

Contract Award

Contract Negotiation

Cost Estimating

Crew Scheduling & Management

Critical Path Method (CPM) Scheduling

Density

Depreciation

Design & Engineering

Divestiture

Economic Analysis

Economic Development

Engineering Change Orders (ECOs)

Environmental Engineering

Estimation

Facilities Engineering

Feasibility Analysis

Field Construction Management

Flood Plain

Framing

Geographic Information System (GIS)

Geological Engineering

Historic Renovation

Industrial Development

Infrastructure Development

Inspections

Labor Cost Control

Land Development

Land Planning & Management

Land-Use Studies

Land Valuation

Mapping

Master Scheduling

Model Home

Multi-Use Property

Planned Community

Plat

Portfolio Management

Project Development

Project Management

Project Scheduling

Property Development

Real Estate Development

Real Estate Investment Trust (REIT)

Real Property

Regulatory Compliance & Reporting

Renovation

Reserve Funding

Residential Development

Return on Assets (ROA)

Return on Investment (ROI)

Schematics

Site Development

Site Remediation

Soil Engineering

Specifications

Structural Engineering

Survey

Syndication

Tax Laws

Turnkey Construction

Urban Planning

Value Analysis

Value Comparison

Zoning Bylaws

Zoning Regulations

Jonathan Hardy

Seattle, WA • 216-538-2474 • jonhardy@gmail.com

CONSTRUCTION MANAGER: Design, Engineering & Construction—Worldwide

• **Project Manager:** Directed 20+ turnkey projects from initial planning and proposal stage through entire design, engineering, and construction cycle, to staffing and facilities start-up.

• **Business Leader:** Repeatedly identified and implemented strategies to reduce costs, strengthen customer relationships, improve business processes, and drive profitable growth.

• **Technical Expert:** Maintain up-to-date knowledge of the latest technologies, processes, systems, and advances affecting all phases of the construction industry.

PROFESSIONAL EXPERIENCE

ENVIROSOURCE CONSTRUCTION *($100M global construction company)*   Bellevue, WA—2006 to Present

Senior Project Manager (2012–Present) • **Project Manager** (2009–2012) • **Project Engineer** (2006–2009)

Manage large-scale construction projects throughout the Pacific Northwest and internationally, with full responsibility for:

• Project Proposals & Presentations	• Design & Engineering	• Estimating
• Project Control & Management	• Purchasing & Materials	• Construction
• Human Resources & Training	• Trade Union Negotiations	• Contracts
• Contract Administration	• CPM Scheduling	• Budgeting
• Subcontract Administration	• Field Project Management	• Licensing

Achievements & Project Highlights:

• Delivered more than **20** major turnkey design, engineering, and construction projects—completing more than **$300M** in projects at **$30.5M** under budget. Achieved or surpassed all cost, schedule, quality, and performance objectives.

• Reduced departmental staffing from **80** to **40** and maintained stable workforce through the use of both permanent and job-shop personnel. Cross-trained staff to optimize performance.

• Partnered with key suppliers and reduced annual purchasing costs by up to **$100K**.

• Successfully managed the company's first international project, a **$12M** venture in the Czech Republic. Brought project from concept through design and construction to start-up in cooperation with a Czech, Japanese, and US workforce.

• Introduced leading-edge design and engineering technologies, including complete conversion from manual to AutoCAD systems. Reduced time requirements by **50%**.

ZSUN OIL COMPANY *(Industrial/chemical refinery)*   Everett, WA— 2004–2006

Project Engineer

• Completed backlog of **35** projects within first **6** months.

• Designed and built a **$500K** facility **6** weeks ahead of schedule and **$350K** below budget

HK JACKSON, INC. *(Prime contractor for startup of $12.5M Anheuser-Busch brewery)*   Seattle, WA—2003–2004

Construction Engineer

EDUCATION	**MSCE—Construction Management**, University of Washington
	BSCE—Structural Engineering, University of Southern California
CERTIFICATIONS	Quality Assurance Certification in Nondestructive Testing
	Certification in Hazardous Waste Handling
AFFILIATIONS	American Society of Construction Engineers
	American Institute of Structural Engineers

To: Info@FanfareConstruction.com
From: David Rodriguez
Subject: Licensed Contractor Opportunity

With a 15-year history of never missing a construction project deadline, I have proven skills and a track record of performance that can benefit your company.

My experience encompasses every aspect of design–build residential projects from a few thousand dollars to more than $1 million. To be certain to meet deadlines—without driving up costs—I have mastered a few fundamental skills and use them on every job:

- Planning and Scheduling: Creating a schedule that is "do-able" and coordinating all of the moving pieces so that construction stays on track.
- Monitoring the Critical Path: Identifying and eliminating any roadblocks that do occur very early in the process.
- Troubleshooting: Bringing creative, resourceful thinking to solve field problems and move projects forward.
- Teambuilding: Creating the right atmosphere on the building site by valuing all workers and encouraging collaboration rather than competition.

In addition to years of hands-on experience, I have a degree in Construction Management and a Contractor's License from the State of Ohio. I stay up to date with trends and advances—new materials, new technologies, new processes, and other changes that affect the building industry. My greatest satisfaction comes from doing a job well, on time, and on budget.

I would appreciate the opportunity to meet with you to discuss your needs and my background in more detail. I am confident you will agree I have the experience, know-how, and attitude you are seeking.

Sincerely,

David Rodriguez
>>>>>>>>>>
216-345-1110
davidrodriguez98@gmail.com

Keyword Answers to Interview Questions

Tell me about yourself.

As a project manager with Baywater Development, I hold full profit and loss responsibility for the construction of mixed-use retail and commercial facilities throughout the state of Virginia. Over the past five years, I've managed more than 25 projects with budgets ranging from $250,000 to more than $5 million and worksite crews of up to 200 each day. Twenty-four of those projects were delivered on time and within budget; the remaining project was halted due to environmental remediation issues that arose during final inspection.

I have an expert knowledge of building codes and regulations, all building trades, competitive bidding, contract administration, and owner/investor relations. Most important, I'm an intensely hard worker, and I love the many challenges in property development and construction. Your current projects sound most interesting, and I'm eager to learn more.

What is the most valuable skill you bring to our company?

The reason that I've been able to deliver all of my projects on time and within budget is because of my strong planning and organizational skills. When I have 200 people on a project, a hundred phone calls a day, and more than a thousand other things to juggle, it is critical that I be able to quickly and accurately prioritize what needs to be done, when, and by whom. This is, by far, the most valuable skill I bring to you and to your projects.

What is your most significant achievement?

In 2014, I was asked to take over a project that had some serious challenges. Costs were way over budget, project scheduling was a disaster, contracts were never signed, and the real estate developers were ready to pull out. That's what I encountered my first day on the job.

The next day I assembled everyone, from the design architects to the road paving crews, and outlined an entirely new construction plan. Six months later the project was delivered and the facility opened on time. In fact, because of my efforts and those of my crew, my company received a sizable construction bonus.

Chapter 7

Customer Service

Top 100 Keywords

Account Administration

Account Relationship
  Management

Account Service

Benefits & Features

Billing

Branding

Budgeting

Business Administration

Buying Trends

Call Center

Claims Administration

Client

Client Communications

Client Presentations

Client Retention

Communications

Complaint Resolution

Corporate Identity

Corporate Image

Cost Containment

Customer Communications

Customer Development

Customer Focus Groups

Customer Loyalty

Customer Management

Customer Needs Assessment

Customer Outreach

Customer Relations

Customer Relationship
  Management

Customer Retention

Customer Satisfaction

Customer Service

Customer Support

Customer Transactions

Data Collection & Analysis

Data Reporting

E-Commerce

Electronic Orders

Field Service Operations

Focus Groups

Fulfillment

Graphic Design

Inbound Service Operations

Incentives

Information Technology

Inventory Control

Key Account Relationship
    Management

Key Accounts

Member Retention

Member Services

Membership

Merchandise Management

Merchandising

Newsletters

Offline Order Processing

Online Communications

Online Order Processing

Order Fulfillment

Organization

Outbound Service Operation

Payment Processing

Performance Improvement

Policies & Procedures

Pricing

Print Communications

Prioritization

Problem Resolution

Process Simplification

Product Launch

Product Management

Product Specifications

Products

Project Administration

Projects

Quality

Quality Benchmark

Recordkeeping

Relationship Management

Reporting

Retail

Retention

Sales Administration

Service Benchmarks

Service Delivery

Service Measures

Service Quality

Services

Social Media

Statistical Analysis

Surveys

Team Building

Telecommunications

Telemarketing

Telephone Support

Telesales

Training & Development

Transaction Processing

Virtual Administration

Website Management

Wholesale Accounts

Noreen Collins

noreen.r.collins@comcast.net   (415) 548-9721   www.linkedin.com/in/noreenrcollins

Customer Service / Consumer Affairs / Response Center Management

*Built 2 high-profile customer response and customer management organizations
that consistently exceeded productivity, quality and customer satisfaction objectives.*

- Strategic Business Planning
- Technology Acquisition
- Vendor Sourcing / Negotiations
- Contract Development / Compliance
- Market Research / Analysis

- Customer / Client Service Management
- Multi-Site Call Center Management
- Human Resource Allocation
- Professional Training & Development
- Process / Procedure Standardization

Professional Experience

SIMPSON FOODS, San Francisco, CA • 2003–Present

Fast-track career leading nationwide customer service and customer response operations of one of the largest food manufacturers in the US. Honored with distinguished corporate performance awards, including:

- Above and Beyond The Call Of Duty (2015)
- TQM Team of the Quarter (2010 and 2013)
- Consumer Affairs Award for Continued Excellent Performance (2011 and 2012)
- Consumer Affairs Award of Excellence (2009 and 2010)

Operations Manager—Customer Response Information Services • 2013–Present
15 direct reports • 150 vendor-based contractors • 2.5M annual calls • $8M annual operating budget

One of only 3 professionals retained following transition from in-house to outsourced customer service operation. Retained accountability as Operations Manager (since 2008) while shifting focus to a 9-site organization (2 large contracted centers and 7 remote, in-house centers). Negotiate vendor contracts and monitor vendor compliance with metrics for call volume, call duration, productivity, documentation, and customer satisfaction.

- Led smooth transition from in-house to outsourced operation. Met **100%** of target dates and milestones.

- Reduced cost per contact by **25%** in 2 years with long-term projections indicating further reductions in both call and email response costs.

- Wrote complete business plan to standardize all policies and procedures (coupon refunds, shipping, claims processing, nutritional information) and provide contractors with a single operational reference manual.

- Designed and directed a **30-hour** training program at vendor site. Educated personnel in Simpson standards, quality objectives, customer satisfaction, and **3000+** products.

Noreen Collins • Page 2

noreen.r.collins@comcast.net   (415) 548-9721   www.linkedin.com/in/noreenrcollins

Operations Manager — Customer Response Information Center • 2009–2013
80 staff • $4.8M annual budget

Promoted to start up and manage an integrated, full-service customer response and fulfillment center. Established strategic plans and operating goals, designed departmental infrastructure, determined staffing and technology requirements, and created policies/procedures for all facets of service management. Coordinated crisis communications and national product recalls.

- Built internal customer response organization from ground floor into a nationwide operation servicing more than **1M** customers annually.

- Transitioned customer response from a function that had been scattered throughout the company into a cohesive and accountable work group. Reduced costs per contract by **60%** and average issue resolution time from **21+** days to **3.**

- Wrote business plan and led introduction of voice response technology. Co-directed project from initial feasibility and cost analysis through vendor sourcing and final implementation.

- Devised an employee hotline to obtain recommendations for productivity and quality improvements. Reduced operating costs by more than **$500K.**

- Led internal training programs to enhance staff capabilities in communications, customer management, problem resolution, and issue documentation. Created a forum for the ongoing exchange of information between all core operating functions.

With executive management team, developed strategy to transition to outsourced consumer response operations. Directed complete downsizing of internal department and accepted new assignment directing the contracted operation.

Customer Information Analyst • 2007–2009

Served as direct liaison between Customer Response Information Center and Marketing, Quality Assurance, Legal, and Manufacturing. Translated information regarding consumer issues, trends, and market opportunities to support diverse product development, design, packaging, distribution, and promotional efforts. Conducted detailed analyses of consumer data, identified and researched complaints, and resolved issues impacting consumer purchasing/satisfaction.

Senior Home Economist / Chef • 2004–2007
Development Technologist • 2003–2004

Promoted within 9 months to senior product development position providing critical technical, culinary, and consumer expertise to lead expansion of Simpson's product portfolio.

Education

MS, Institutional Management, University of San Francisco, 2011
BS, Food & Nutrition, Florida A&M University, 2003

Professional Activities

Member—Society of Consumer Affairs Professionals, Incoming Call Center Management, 2010–Present
Presenter—"Training & Hiring," Customer Service Organization National Conference, 2014

José Maldonado

Miami, FL 33389
305-845-2837
josemaldonado@gmail.com

March 5, 2016

John Garber
Biscayne Bay Distributors, Inc.
5600 Seminole Avenue
Miami, FL 33827

Dear Mr. Garber:

Your East Coast district manager, Jay Singh, suggested that I contact you regarding your current opening for a Customer Service Manager. Jay knows of my work ethic and customer service skills through his prior employment at Pepsi and believes that I would be a valuable addition to the team at Biscayne Bay.

My professional and personal qualifications include:

- Three years in progressively responsible account management roles with Pepsi.
- Experience coordinating cross-functional customer service and support teams.
- Outstanding performance in building and managing customer relationships.
- Outgoing personality with strong communication, problem-solving, and decision-making skills.
- Ability to independently manage time, customer commitments, and resources.
- Four-year college degree with solid academic performance and outstanding athletic achievements.

I am impressed with what Jay has told me about Biscayne Bay's dedication to customers as the key to its growth. That is precisely the environment where I thrive and where I can add the most value. I will follow up with you early next week to see if we might schedule a time to meet.

Sincerely,

José Maldonado

Keyword Answers to Interview Questions

Tell me about yourself.

Building positive customer relationships is what I do best. Whether working to service an existing customer account, resolve a customer service problem, or develop systems to streamline and enhance customer service operations, I have consistently exceeded all service and retention objectives.

Equally important is my success in training other customer service professionals in communications, project management, customer relationship management, and customer retention. To date, I have earned three commendations from Sprint for "excellence in customer service management" and a corporate award for "employee training and development." In addition, I was featured in Sprint's quarterly employee magazine as one of the "Top 10 Customer Service Associates" in the corporation.

I've dedicated my career to customer service, with great results for each company and great satisfaction for me. Now, I'm eager for the next step in my career.

What is the most valuable skill you bring to our company?

Communications and interpersonal relations are my strongest skills and the foundation for my success in customer service management. I really do enjoy people and find that I'm able to quickly build rapport and establish relationships.

I value my customers, and I want them to know that. When I tell them I'll call back, I do. When I tell them I'll research a problem and resolve it, I do. When I tell them I'll email them information, I do. I execute, I follow through, and my customers always appreciate the effort.

What is your most significant achievement?

Over the past three years, I've trained more than 50 newly hired customer service representatives for Sprint's Regional Operations Center. I'm most proud of the fact that 47 of them are still with the company and that 12 of them have been promoted to supervisory positions.

This clearly demonstrates that not only can I manage customer service operations with excellent results, I can also train others to perform equally well in challenging, fast-paced situations.

Chapter 8

Engineering

Top 100 Keywords

Aeronautical Engineering

Audio Engineering

Automotive Engineering

Benchmark

Biological Engineering

Biomedical Engineering

Broadcast Engineering

Budgeting

Capital Project

Ceramic Engineering

Chemical Engineering

Civil Engineering

Commissioning

Computer-Aided Design (CAD)

Computer-Aided Manufacturing (CAM)

Computer Engineering

Cost Analysis

Cross-Functional Team

Customer Management

Data Collection & Analysis

Design Specifications

Development Engineering

Efficiency Improvement

Electrical Engineering

Electronics Engineering

Energy Engineering

Engineering Change Order (ECO)

Engineering Documentation

Environmental Engineering

Ergonomic Techniques

Experimental Design

Experimental Methods

Facilities Engineering

Fault Analysis

Field Performance

Final Customer Acceptance

Genetics Engineering

Hardware Engineering

Industrial Engineering

Industrial Hygiene

Information Technology

Maintenance Engineering

Manpower Planning

Manufacturing Engineering

Manufacturing Integration

Marine Engineering

Materials Engineering

Mechanical Engineering

Methods Design

Mining Engineering

Networks

Nuclear Engineering

Occupational Safety & Health
    Administration (OSHA)

Oceanographic Engineering

Offshore Engineering

Operating & Maintenance (O&M)

Operations Research

Optical Engineering

Outsourcing

Performance Improvement

Petroleum Engineering

Planetary Engineering

Plant Engineering

Process Development

Process Engineering

Process Standardization

Product Design

Product Development Cycle

Product Functionality

Product Innovation

Product Lifecycle Management

Product Manufacturability

Product Reliability

Productivity Improvement

Project Planning & Management

Projects

Prototype

Quality

Quality Engineering

Regulatory Compliance

Reliability Engineering

Research & Development
    (R&D)

Resource Management

Root Cause Analysis

Scale-Up

Site Management

Software Engineering

Specifications

Standards

Statistical Analysis

Structural Engineering

Systems Engineering

Systems Integration

Technical Briefings

Technical Liaison Affairs

Technology

Telecommunications Engineering

Test Engineering

Training & Development

Work Methods Analysis

Mark Bernard

Mesa, AZ • 480-890-1120
markbernard@gmail.com
www.linkedin.com/in/markbernard

DESIGN, ENGINEERING & MANUFACTURING

Advanced Information, Telecommunications & Electronic Packaging Technologies
Expertise in Team Building, Productivity/Efficiency Gain, Quality & Resource Maximization

CORE COMPETENCIES

- Product Design & Mechanical Engineering
- Project Planning & Management
- Reliability & Performance Analysis
- Automated Design Technologies
- Concurrent Design & Engineering

- Production & Assembly Operations
- Product Cost & Production Scheduling
- Materials Planning & Management
- Product Testing & Prototyping
- Customer Presentations & Negotiations

PROFESSIONAL EXPERIENCE

Engineering Manager (Section Supervisor)   2011–Present
Space Inc., Mesa, AZ

Senior Engineering Manager with full responsibility for strategic planning, staffing, budgeting and technical performance of all power control electronic system design projects. Lead team of 15 professional engineers throughout entire project cycle, from initial design through prototype, test, quality, and transition to full-scale production.

- Manage $4M in annual project budgets. Completed 10+ projects over 5 years with total cost exceeding $30M.
- Coordinate production planning and scheduling, purchasing, and subcontracting. Provide engineering expertise to internal and outsourced manufacturing teams involved in supply/material management.
- Lead technical presentations to major customers nationwide for both new contracts and renewals. Instrumental in winning more than $1.2B in contract awards.
- Spearhead project teams responsible for the redesign and improved manufacturability of existing products and technologies.
- Coordinate the selection and integration of advanced technologies for project design, vibration and thermal analysis, scheduling, systems integration, and other core functions.

PERFORMANCE HIGHLIGHTS

- Built a talented and technically proficient mechanical engineering team successful in delivering cost-effective, high-performance designs, products, and technologies.
- Delivered $500K annual cost savings through redesign of assembly processes for a major systems component.
- Reduced component volume 70% by implementing custom hybrid circuits and surface mounts.
- Established company-wide standard practices for all mechanical engineering processes, methods, and documentation. Created and led a robust design review process.

Mark Bernard
480-890-1120 • markbernard@gmail.com

Engineering Manager   2007–2011
Greinert Systems, Palo Alto, CA

Recruited back to previous employer to manage sophisticated mechanical engineering group designing mobile, collapsible antenna systems for deployment worldwide. Led a team of 7 professional engineers and up to $1M in annual project budgets.

- Selected as Mechanical Design Project Leader for a multimillion-dollar project. Managed cost, schedule, and technical performance of reconfigured rack-mounted ESM equipment that became a mainstay of the business due to exceptional product performance and durability.

Engineering Specialist   2003–2007
Litton-Applied Technology, Sunnyvale, CA

Lead Engineer for more than $800K annually in systems design projects, ranging from computer components to advanced digital and RF electronics. Concurrent responsibility for the design evaluation and oversight of power supply and microwave device subcontractors.

- Earned "Top Performer" award for contributions to a time-sensitive, critical product update.

Senior Engineer   2000–2003
Greinert Systems, Palo Alto, CA

Produced mechanical and environmentally resistant designs for sophisticated, high-vibration applications. Assisted in project budgeting, scheduling, task definition, team supervision, and technical support.

- Appointed Cost Proposal Manager for large RFP.
- Doubled yield of high-voltage magnetics in production through product and process redesign.

EDUCATION

MS Engineering Management, University of California—Los Angeles, 2010
MS Mechanical Engineering, University of California—Santa Cruz, 2003
BS Mechanical Engineering, *Magna Cum Laude*, University of San Francisco, 2000

PERSONAL PROFILE

Two-year tour of duty with the US Army. Honorably discharged.
Design and assemble custom golf clubs as a small, independent venture.
Play tournament golf through Arizona Golf Association (AGA).

To: Jobs@PrinceLabs.com
From: Christina Lawrence
Re: Environmental Coordinator—Job Posting #NC–24536

With 13 years of experience in Environmental Engineering, I bring to Prince Laboratories an in-depth knowledge of environmental issues, regulations, and compliance impacting chemical and industrial manufacturing.

Offering deep expertise in resource recovery and conservation, I have:

- Completed 100+ remediation projects, including dozens of Superfund sites.
- Developed extensive knowledge of soil, air, and groundwater remediation systems and technologies.
- Designed environmental systems for hazardous waste, hazardous materials, air emissions, and wastewater discharges.

In managing challenging projects, I have become known for resolving long-standing environmental issues, achieving compliance with state and federal regulations, and reducing the costs associated with environmental engineering and remediation. Further, I have worked closely with management teams to guide acquisition, divestiture, and product development efforts.

Your Environmental Coordinator posting seems tailor-made for my talents, interests, and experience. I would appreciate the opportunity to learn more about the position and share further details of my background that I believe will be of significant value to Prince Labs. Thank you in advance for your time and consideration.

Christina Lawrence
========================
chris.lawrence@yahoo.com
312-671-1210

Keyword Answers to Interview Questions

Tell me about yourself.

My most distinguishing characteristic is that I have Master's Degrees in both Mechanical Engineering and Electrical Engineering. This places me in a uniquely qualified position as a senior facilities engineer, able to manage large-scale plant design, construction, scale-up, and production operations.

For most of my career I've held dual roles, responsible for both facilities design and engineering as well as new product development. In addition, I have a wealth of experience in technical documentation, technical communications, project management, methods design, process development, and OSHA reporting.

Your current opening seems like a great fit for this diversity of experience, so I am excited to talk to you today.

What is the most valuable skill you bring to our company?

My most valuable skill is the breadth of my engineering experience, including my expertise in both mechanical and electrical engineering, as well as my work experience in systems engineering, process engineering, HVAC, and systems integration.

Because of this broad experience, I can quickly and accurately evaluate the requirements for complete projects, determining what personnel, technologies, engineering systems, finances, and other resources will be required to achieve project milestones.

In addition, and again because of the wide range of my experience, I am able to effectively communicate with personnel from every engineering discipline.

What is your most significant achievement?

Last year, our plant experienced a major fire that devastated the production floor while doing significant damage to the warehouse and loading docks. In cooperation with five other engineers, I was given lead responsibility for getting the plant back up and running.

With more than 100 workers on the site each day, we rebuilt the production area, designed and installed all new electrical and HVAC systems, and renovated all damaged areas. Most significant, the project was completed in 120 days and we achieved all customer delivery objectives.

Chapter 9

Equipment Installation, Maintenance, and Repair

Top 100 Keywords

Agricultural Equipment

Alignment

Analysis Instrumentation

Applied Physics

Apprenticeship

Assembly

Automotive Equipment

Aviation Equipment

Avionics Equipment

Biomedical Equipment & Technology

Blueprints

Calibration

Circuitry

Commercial Equipment

Component-Level Repair

Computer-Aided Design (CAD)

Computer Systems & Technology

Computerized Controls

Configuration

Construction Equipment

Control Systems

Critical Systems

Data Collection & Analysis

Debugging

Defects

Diagnostic Instrumentation

Diagnostic Testing

Diagnostics

Diagrams

Electric Equipment & Systems

Electrical Engineering

Electro-Mechanical Equipment

Electronic Equipment & Systems

Engineering

Engines

Fault Isolation

Field Engineering

Field Service

Fleet Management

Hand Tools

Hazardous Materials (HAZMAT)

Heating, Ventilating & Air
  Conditioning (HVAC)

Heavy Equipment

Hydraulics

Industrial Controls

Industrial Engineering

Industrial Machinery

Inspection

Installation

Instrumentation

Inventory Planning & Control

Logic Analysis

Lubrication

Machine Design

Machinery

Maintenance

Maintenance Engineering

Manuals

Materials

Mathematics

Mechanical Engineering

Mechanical Systems

Mechanics

Medical Equipment

Multimeter

Network Systems

Office Equipment

Ohmmeter

Operating Manuals

Overhaul

Parts

Power Source

Power Tools

Precision Instrumentation

Preventive Maintenance

Programmable Logic Controller
  (PLC)

Radio Systems

Records & Reporting

Repair

Rigging

Schematics

Service Manuals

Shop Mechanics

Software

Specifications

Statistical Process Control
  (SPC)

Statistics

Technical Training

Technology Systems

Telecommunications Systems

Test Equipment

Testing

Tooling

Troubleshooting

Vending Machines

Vibration Analysis

Voltmeter

Welding

Wiring

Work Orders

Jamal Wilkins

312-555-7120 • jamalwilkins@gmail.com

MAINTENANCE TECHNICIAN & SUPERVISOR
Commercial & Industrial Buildings & Facilities

Conscientious and customer-focused maintenance professional with advanced knowledge of facilities equipment and systems. Talent for troubleshooting—solving small problems before they impact productivity—and a consistent record of on-time, on-budget project completion.

- HVAC
- Electrical Systems
- ISO 14001 Procedures
- Building Automation Controls
- Subcontractor Selection & Management
- Building Analysis & Troubleshooting
- Project Management
- Proposal Development
- Staff Supervision

PROFESSIONAL EXPERIENCE

MIDWEST BUILDING TECHNOLOGIES, Chicago, IL   2013–2016

Facilities Maintenance Technician

Placed in charge of new account, providing outsourced facilities maintenance for Synoverse Technologies—400,000 square feet of manufacturing and office space in 2 locations with $100K annual maintenance budget. Prepared proposals, supervised staff and subcontractors, and managed projects start to finish.

- Ran a lean operation, managing the facilities with a staff of 3 while previously Synoverse had used 15.
- Scheduled and completed all building repairs, preventative maintenance, and troubleshooting for HVAC equipment and systems, including:

    - 1200 Tons of Chillers
    - 400-hp Boilers
    - Emergency Generators
    - Fire Pumps
    - Johnson Controls Metasys DDC Controls Systems
    - Fire & Life Safety Systems
    - Liebert UPS Systems
    - Electrical & Plumbing Systems

- Saved $6K annually in chemical costs by proposing and carrying out a project to automate antiquated, inefficient chemical-injection system in the cooling tower.
- Documented all work activities in accordance with ISO 14001 procedures. Prepared reports for senior management, improving reporting by developing new forms and documents using MS Word and Excel.
- Consistently achieved excellent customer satisfaction scores.

NORTH SHORE HEATING & AIR CONDITIONING, Evanston, IL   2009–2013

HVAC Service Technician

Troubleshot, maintained, and repaired HVAC equipment including rooftop package units up to 75 tons, split A/C systems, gas- and oil-fired boilers and furnaces, centrifugal and screw-type chillers, cooling towers, computer room A/C systems, and fan box systems.

TRAINING & CERTIFICATION

Air Conditioning/Refrigeration Electro-Mechanical Technologies
- The Refrigeration School, Inc., Chicago, IL
- Honor Graduate, 99% Grade Average

Certifications & Licenses
- EPA Refrigerant Certified UNIVERSAL (through ACCA and Illinois State University)
- Electrical HVAC/RFRG License (State of Illinois)
- Gas Heating Mechanic License (City of Chicago)
- Gas Fitter License (City of Chicago)
- Class D-2 Warm Air Heating Mechanic Apprenticeship (State of Illinois)

To: Marie.Fallon@SkillSearch.com
From: patcorales@aol.com
Re: Skilled Mechanic (Indeed.com Job Posting)

Dear Ms. Fallon:

I am very interested in your available Mechanic position and would like to have the opportunity demonstrate that I am the right person for the job.

People say that I can fix anything. While that might not be totally true, I do have a wide range of skills that can help keep equipment and facilities running smoothly and safely.

My entire career has involved building, fixing, and maintaining equipment for manufacturing and construction companies. I improve my strong mechanical aptitude with regular training, a resourceful attitude, and the willingness to tackle just about anything.

The attached resume describes my experience, but it cannot convey the creativity and energy I bring to every job nor the satisfaction I get from making machinery and equipment run well.

I will follow up on Friday and hope that we can meet soon. Thank you for your consideration.

Sincerely,

Pat Corales
****

patcorales@aol.com
203-467-1276 (Cell – call or text anytime)

Keyword Answers to Interview Questions

Tell me about yourself.

I've worked as a machinist and production operator for eight years for John Deere at one of its largest contracted manufacturing facilities in Michigan. When I look back on my first day on the job compared to what I can do now, it's a huge leap forward in machining skills, technology skills, efficiency and productivity, and overall production operations.

In addition to learning on the job, I've completed a number of technical training programs and certifications that have strengthened both my hands-on tech and engineering skills and my workplace skills—things like project management, inventory control, training, and quality assurance.

On a personal note, I'm active in our local Moose Lodge, enjoy snowboarding and other outdoor activities, and volunteer each year with several organizations that John Deere sponsors.

What is the most valuable skill you bring to our company?

I would say that my #1 skill is machining, because I enjoy it so much and I'm one of the most talented machinists in my organization. A lot of machining is focused on problem resolution. For example, it might be that one part of our manufacturing line is encountering bottlenecks and stoppages on a regular basis. My co-workers and I will troubleshoot to identify what we can do to eliminate the problem by creating and machining new production components to meet our performance and quality objectives.

It's always so fulfilling to walk out on the floor—six months after we've redone a component—and watch assembly line operations working flawlessly.

What is your most significant achievement?

I've already addressed my success as a machinist, so I'll focus on the achievements I've helped bring about in the capabilities of my co-workers. Despite the fact that I've been with Deere for only eight years, I'm one of the most senior machinists in the organization and, as a result, I'm also the one who's always called on to train and support new employees.

I've trained more than 20 people in the past few years, 18 of whom still work for Deere and are performing to or above our productivity and quality standards. I like to think that my training has helped these people in their careers, and I'm quite proud of that achievement.

Chapter 10

Finance and Economics

Top 100 Keywords

Acquisition

Amortization

Asset Management

Asset Purchase

Asset Valuation

Board of Directors

Chapter 7 Bankruptcy

Chapter 11 Bankruptcy

Commercial Banking

Commercial Credit

Commercial Paper

Corporate Development

Corporate Finance

Corporate Governance

Corporate Taxation

Cost-Benefit Economics

Data Collection & Analysis

Debt Financing

Divestiture

Earnings Before Interest & Tax (EBIT)

Econometrics

Economic Modeling

Economics

Equity Financing

Excel

Feasibility Analysis

Financial Accounting

Financial Analysis & Reporting

Financial Controls

Financial Economics

Financial Examination

Financial Instruments

Financial Modeling

Financial Planning

Financial Reserves

Financial Services

Financial Transactions

Foreign Exchange (FX)

Forensic Economics

Funds Management

Global Financial Markets

Industrial Economics

Information Systems

Information Technology

Initial Public Offering (IPO)

Interest-Bearing Instrument

Internal Revenue Service (IRS)

International Economics

International Finance

International Monetary Fund (IMF)

Investment Management

Investor Relations

Joint Venture

Leveraged Buy-Out (LBO)

Liability Management

Limited Liability Corporation (LLC)

Line of Credit

Macroeconomics

Monetary Policy

Management Buy-Out (MBO)

Management Reporting

Margin Improvement

Mathematical Modeling

Merger

Microeconomics

Monetary Policy

Money Market

Partnership

Pension Plan Administration

Portfolio Analysis & Management

Private Equity

Profit & Loss (P&L) Management

Profit Sharing Plan Administration

Profitability Analysis

Project Economics

Project Management

Regulatory Compliance & Reporting

Regulatory Standards

Return on Assets (ROA)

Return on Equity (ROE)

Return on Investment (ROI)

Risk Management & Control

Road Show Presentations

Sarbanes-Oxley (SOX)

Securities & Exchange Commission (SEC)

Shareholder Relations

Statistical Analysis & Reporting

Statistical Modeling

Stock Purchase

Stockholder Reporting

Strategic Planning

Tax Laws & Legislation

Tax Planning

Tax Shelter

Team Building & Leadership

Technology

Treasury

Trust Funds

Underwriting

Valuation

Venture Capital Financing

MAHESH RAO

503-335-9832 ~ Portland, OR 98326
mahesh.rao@navigator.com ~ www.LinkedIn.com/in/maheshrao

SENIOR FINANCE EXECUTIVE

Corporate Planning ~ Financial Analysis ~ Financial Reporting ~ Treasury ~ Credit Management
Mergers & Acquisitions ~ Joint Ventures ~ Strategic Marketing Partnerships ~ Creative Leadership

Member of senior management team of several high-growth, high-tech corporations. Contributed millions of dollars in revenues and profits through achievements in debt and equity management, operating cost reduction, market development, contract negotiations, and general business management.

EDUCATION AND CERTIFICATION

1999	**Certified Management Accountant (CMA)**
1998	**MBA**, University of Washington
1996	**BS / Business & Finance**, Seattle Pacific University

EXECUTIVE EXPERIENCE

Principal—2014 to Present

NAVIGATOR NETWORK, Portland, OR
(Firm providing consulting services and interim executive leadership for strategic business planning, finance, investment acquisition, marketing, technology development, and organizational change.)

➤ **Interim CFO** of Greene Video (media post-production company), representing their interests in complex acquisition by MultiMedia Company (entertainment group that just completed $50M+ IPO). Introduced the parties and negotiated key elements of acquisition agreement among owners, attorneys, and financial counsel. Devoted 9 months to managing financial and operations reorganization prior to acquisition.

  • Restored credibility throughout the banking, credit, and vendor communities.
  • Restructured more than $8M in corporate debt.
  • Negotiated and resolved complex IRS issues, saving $300K in penalty liabilities.

➤ **Finance & Marketing Consultant,** US Capital, a premier provider of capital equipment acquisition and leasing services, and business partner of my previous employer. Retained to launch the start-up of sales, marketing, and business development programs throughout the Western US.

  • Delivered significant financial contracts and sales transactions. Closed $5M in one year.
  • Structured, negotiated, and closed leasing transactions between technology providers (Philips, Symons, Sony, Discreet Logic) and financial institutions.

Director of Finance & Administration—2011–2014

SYMONS TELEVISION SYSTEMS, INC., San Francisco, CA
($100M manufacturer of electronic broadcast equipment for networks and cable systems worldwide.)

➤ Recruited as **Manager of Credit & Financial Services** for the marketing, sales, and field service organization supporting operations in North America, South America, and the Pacific Rim. Promoted to **Director of Finance & Administration** for the group within first year and given full responsibility for accounting, MIS, sales administration, HR, and operations. Managed 20 staff.

MAHESH RAO   503-335-9832 ~ mahesh.rao@navigator.com

SYMONS TELEVISION SYSTEMS, INC. *(Continued):*

- Established new operating division to fund customer acquisitions. Negotiated strategic partnerships with lending institution and third-party agent for funding, finance administration, and collection. In 2 years, business unit grew to $44M in annual sales.
- Rewrote corporate credit policy, centralized collections, and improved receivables 20 days. Consulted with legal staff in Argentina to develop strategic plans for recovery of $1M+ in past-due receivables.

Chief Financial Officer / Executive Vice President—2006–2011

LINTEK, INC., Cadwell, OR
(High-growth manufacturer of high-tech underwater electrical systems.)

➤ **Senior Finance Executive** directing corporate finance, accounting, credit, treasury, tax, shareholder relations, venture capital negotiations, and lease/contract negotiations. Held concurrent executive management responsibility for business development, marketing, and operations.

- Restructured corporate debt and increased company net worth by more than 100%.
- Negotiated financial, legal, and contractual terms for 10-year international license with UK company for technology marketing and distribution. Generated immediate cash and market share.
- Featured in *Wall Street Journal Small Business Report* for negotiation of export financing from the State of Oregon and EXIM Bank to fund Lintek's international business operations. Repaid $1M+ in 2 years.

Chief Operating Officer / Executive Vice President / Board Director—2001–2006

MOUNTAIN REGIONAL BANK, North Peak, CA

➤ **Senior Operating Executive** leading an aggressive reorganization and restructuring of multi-branch banking system to position company for sale. Directed 90 staff in corporate finance and administration, legal, HR, sales/marketing, banking services, lending/credit, customer service, and regulatory affairs.

- Reengineered core processes and delivered long-term gains in profitability and productivity.
- Delivered 25%+ average rate of return on commercial properties.
- Successfully penetrated new market niches and expanded professional clientele.

Administration & Corporate Planning Associate—1998–2001

COASTAL BANK, Los Angeles, CA

PROFESSIONAL ACTIVITIES

Teaching   Guest Lecturer in Finance, Oregon State University
                    Guest Lecturer in Finance, Certified Management Accountants Workshop

Affiliations Broadcast Cable Financial Managers Association (Chair, Membership Committee)

Annemarie Silver

818.438.7971
annemarie.silver@gmail.com

March 5, 2016

Michael Caulfield
Bayside Manufacturing, Inc.
1900 Commercial Way
Bayside, NY 11387

Dear Mr. Caulfield:

Corporate finance is no longer just a "numbers" game. As a Senior Financial Manager with Merlena, my role has extended far beyond finance to include strategic business planning, marketing, new product development, information technology, sales administration, manufacturing, and general operating management within several of the corporation's emerging and high-growth business units.

Initiatives and results have been significant:

- Financial leadership for development and market launch of 3 major product lines that have generated more than **$30 million in new revenues.**

- Reorganization of core business function, delivering **25% staff reduction** with no loss in performance.

- Management of dynamic **$20+ million budgeting process** impacting all major operating units throughout the corporation.

- Coordination of large-scale business operating plans with particular emphasis on financial, capital, marketing, and organizational development components.

My management style is direct and decisive, yet flexible in responding to the constantly changing demands of my staff, management teams, and the marketplace. Most significant is my ability to work across diverse divisions, linking finance with operations to facilitate expansion, reorganization, and operating improvements.

I look forward to speaking with you to further highlight my qualifications and explore your specific financial needs and operating objectives. Thank you.

Sincerely,

Annemarie Silver

Keyword Answers to Interview Questions

Tell me about yourself.

For the past four years, I've worked as a senior financial analyst with Xerox's Business Services Division. Beginning as a junior analyst, I advanced rapidly through several increasingly responsible financial positions to my current assignment.

In this capacity, I am responsible for managing a host of financial functions with an emphasis on data collection, analysis, extrapolation, and reporting. In partnership with a team of more senior-level financial analysts and managers, I work to ensure that the Division operates based on solid financial data for both short-term action and long-range planning.

Further, I have been essential in the introduction of several critical cost-containment programs that improved our bottom-line net earnings by an average of 12% in 2015. Is this the kind of experience you are looking for in your next senior financial analyst?

What is the most valuable skill you bring to our company?

Throughout my professional career, and even in my earlier days while still a college student, I have consistently demonstrated strong analytical, problem-solving, and reasoning skills. Never daunted by a challenge, I have accepted several special projects with my current employer —projects that no one else wanted because of the depth of analytical review required to identify the underlying problems and determine the proper resolution.

To me, analysis is second nature. I thoroughly enjoy the intense research and review that it requires, the often complex mathematical calculations, and most importantly, the ability to deliver findings that create positive change.

What is your most significant achievement?

My most recent notable accomplishment was a $200,000 cost savings I helped to deliver by providing accurate financial data for the renegotiation of several large-dollar service and supplier contracts.

Just as significant have been my contributions to the selection and implementation of a new financial software solution with analytical capabilities far beyond the systems we've used in the past. As a result, I expect that we'll be able to reduce costs by a minimum of $75,000 in operating overhead and administrative costs in 2016, and even more in years to come.

Chapter 11

General Management, Executive Management, and Consulting

Top 100 Keywords

Asset Management

Board of Directors

Brand Management

Budgeting

Business Development

Business Process Reengineering

Capital Projects

Client Engagements

Competitive Market Position

Consensus Building

Consulting

Continuous Process Improvement

Corporate Administration

Corporate Communications

Corporate Culture Change

Corporate Development

Corporate Governance

Corporate Image

Corporate Legal Affairs

Corporate Management

Corporate Mission

Corporate Vision

Cost Reduction

Crisis Communications

Cross-Cultural Communications

Cross-Functional Team
    Leadership

Customer-Driven Management

Customer Loyalty

Customer Retention

Decision-Making

Efficiency Improvement

Emerging Business Ventures

Emerging Markets

Entrepreneurial Leadership

European Economic
    Community (EEC)

Executive Management

Executive Presentations

Financial Management

Financial Restructuring

Funding

General Management

Global Business Development

Global Markets

High-Growth Organization

Infrastructure

Interim Executive

International

Investment Banking

Key Account Relationship Management

Leadership Development

Levcraged Buy-Out

Long-Range Planning

Management Development

Margin Improvement

Market Development

Market-Driven Management

Marketing Management

Matrix Management

Media Strategy

Mergers & Acquisition (M&A)

Multi-Function Experience

Multi-Industry Experience

Multi-Site Operations Management

New Business Development

Operating Infrastructure

Operating Leadership

Organization(al) Culture

Organization(al) Development

Participative Management

Partnerships

Policies & Procedures

Performance Improvement

Presentations

Process Reengineering

Productivity Improvement

Profit & Loss (P&L) Management

Profit Growth

Project Management

Quality Management

Reengineering

Relationship Management

Reorganization

Return-On-Assets (ROA)

Return-On-Equity (ROE)

Return-On-Investment (ROI)

Revenue Growth

Sales Leadership

Service Design/Delivery

Signatory Authority

Start-Up Venture

Strategic Partnership

Strategic Planning

Tactical Planning

Team Building & Leadership

Technology

Telecommunications

Transition Management

Turnaround

Venture Capital

World-Class Organization

ALEXANDER ORTIZ

New York Metro

516-248-8882   www.LinkedIn.com/in/AlexOrtiz   alex.ortiz@mac.com

MANAGEMENT PROFILE

Change agent, innovator, and pioneer in quality management and performance improvement. Expert in building. mentoring, motivating, and leading high-performance teams to achieve aggressive goals.

15+ Years Management Experience in:

- Business Strategy & Strategic Planning
- Financial Management & Risk Assessment
- Regional Sales & Customer Service Operations
- Budgeting & Cost Reduction & Avoidance
- Business Process Automation & Simplification

- Multi-Site Operations Management
- Multicultural Team Building & Leadership
- Strategic & Tactical Market Development
- Call Center Operations Management
- Executive Negotiations & Presentations

PROFESSIONAL EXPERIENCE

AMERICAN TELECOM—NEW YORK METRO & NEW ENGLAND   2000–Present

Sixteen-year management career with one of the nation's largest and most diversified telecommunications corporations. Advanced rapidly through increasingly responsible positions in Customer Sales and Operations, Sales Channel Management, Quality, Regulatory, Finance, Network Services, and Engineering.

Director—NY Business Account Team Centers & ISDN Center (2013–Present)
American Telecom Sales & Service Centers, Garden City, Long Island & Manhattan, NY

Orchestrated the integration of 5 organizations into 1 multifunctional workforce (60+ managers and 340 associates) managing daily sales operations, order provisioning, and billing for the top 15% of revenue-producing business customers throughout the NY metro region. Team services a cross-industry and multiple market-segmented customer base generating $560M in total annual billed revenues.

Manage a $30M annual operating budget, all strategic business planning functions, service delivery, revenue growth, cost management, and employee development and communications operations.

- Built the #1 MegaCenter across the American Telecom New York and New England region.
- Met or exceeded all customer service, corporate, employee satisfaction, call center metrics, and operational objectives in 2013, 2014, and 2015. Currently on target to again exceed all goals in 2016.

Director—Quality Services (2010–2013)
American Telecom Quality Services, Boston, MA

Led a team of 6 quality consultants supporting strategic business units in developing quality improvement plans and programs to accelerate revenue growth, improve customer service, and reduce operating costs. Appointed Corporate Quality Spokesperson.

- Won coveted **American Telecom Team Awards** in 2011 and 2012, achieving 105%–110% of performance metrics for operations and financial gains.
- Conceived, created, and introduced story boards, employee recognition/sharing rallies, and open-space technology sessions to encourage proactive quality improvement initiatives.

ALEXANDER ORTIZ

516-248-8882   Page 2   alex.ortiz@mac.com

AMERICAN TELECOM—continued

Staff Director—Authorized Sales Agents (2008–2010)
American Telecom Sales Channel Management, Boston, MA

As the corporate sales liaison to authorized sales agents throughout New England, challenged to enhance business relationships, develop action-based business plans, strengthen competitive market positioning, improve product and service sales strategies, and drive profitable revenue growth.

- Transitioned lowest ranking agents to first-ever over-quota performance. Closed 2009 at 158% of goal.
- Mentored 2 agents to win the 2008 **Agent of the Year** award and 2009 **Top Agent of Sales Center** award.
- Exceeded personal regional revenue goal by 28%.

Early Professional Career—American Telecom

Staff Director—Regulatory Issues (2006–2008)—MA State Rate Setting & Pricing Strategies
Associate Director—Finance (2004–2006)—Capital Structures, Bond Ratings, Rate of Return, Valuation
Associate Director & Office Manager—Operator Services (2002–2004)—System & Process Automation
Manager—Equipment Installation/Provisioning (2001–2002)—**Exceptional Performance Award**
Loaned Executive—United Way of Central MA (2001)—Corporate Fundraising & Sponsorships
Network Administration Supervisor (2000–2001)—Labor Relations

EDUCATION & PROFESSIONAL DEVELOPMENT

MBA—Finance & Economics (2010)   BABSON COLLEGE/F.W. OLIN GRADUATE SCHOOL
BS—Business Administration & Marketing (2000)   BOSTON UNIVERSITY SCHOOL OF MANAGEMENT
Strategic Quality Management (2002)   UNIVERSITY OF MICHIGAN
Young Executive Development Program (2001)   ASPEN INSTITUTE/FUND FOR CORPORATE INITIATIVES

PROFESSIONAL HONORS & AWARDS

40 Under 40 Award (2010)   BOSTON BUSINESS JOURNAL
YMCA Black Achiever's Award (2008)   GREATER BOSTON YMCA
Fellow, Young Executives Program (2001–Present)   FUND FOR CORPORATE INITIATIVES

PROFESSIONAL AFFILIATIONS & LEADERSHIP ACTIVITIES

BABSON COLLEGE CORPORATION (2010–Present)
Trustee & Board Member / Vice Chair—Marketing & PR Committee / Graduate Advisory Board
Committee on Corporation Members / President's Society / Sir Isaac Newton Society
Volunteer—Career Services / MBA Reunion Committee

GREATER BOSTON YMCA ACHIEVERS PROGRAM (2008–2013)
Volunteer / Workshop Leader / Mentor / Liaison

To: Phillip Carson, President
From: Chris Cannon
Re: Senior Business Manager—Roweson Industries

Dear Mr. Carson:

During 10 years in business and organizational management, I have consistently delivered strong and sustainable performance gains. Most notably, I:

- Reduced headcount 45%, shortened lead times 60%, and improved quality performance 300% for $120M Industrial Products, Inc. (IPI).

- Led the flawless launch of the most successful new product in IPI's history while exceeding $2M in cost reductions and maintaining quality at 99.99%.

- Built the most productive team among 30 teams at 10 plants in 3 countries, applying leadership and communication skills to create a winning culture.

As Senior Business Manager for Roweson, I can provide the manufacturing knowledge and leadership expertise you need to succeed in today's fast-moving environment. I look forward to meeting with you to discuss this opportunity.

Sincerely,

Chris Cannon
****
chris.cannon@mac.com
555-348-1190

Keyword Answers to Interview Questions

Tell me about yourself.

I am the consummate management executive with more than 20 years of senior-level operating management experience. Beginning my career in outside sales and customer relationship management, I was promoted rapidly through a series of increasingly responsible positions—from sales to sales management to regional operations management to my current position as the COO of a $100 million technology services company.

Most notably, I've taken this company from a privately held venture generating $25 million a year to our current status as one of the top five companies in the national market. Much of the company's growth and profitability can be attributed to my strong leadership in providing a sound strategic plan, negotiating critical strategic alliances, leading road shows to obtain financing, and building an operating infrastructure to support accelerated expansion.

It's been a great ride. Now that we've been acquired, I'm interested in putting my skills to work for another company to get similar strong results.

What is the most valuable skill you bring to our company?

Defining a company's mission, creating a clear vision statement, recruiting top management talent, and providing day-to-day operating leadership are the greatest talents I bring to your organization.

Throughout my career, I have been the one responsible for defining each company's model for growth and expansion, its resource requirements, financial needs, personnel needs, and action plan to achieve revenue and profit objectives. And, I have succeeded! As you read my resume, you'll see that in each position I delivered double-digit growth despite intense market competition.

What is your most significant achievement?

When I joined the Axis Company, sales were $25 million a year. Within just five years, my team and I have increased annual sales to more than $100 million with bottom-line profits averaging 22%.

In fact, based on our successful and profitable growth, many of our processes have been benchmarked and incorporated by several of our top competitors. And, as you know, our rapid growth attracted quite a bit of interest in the market and led to Axis being acquired by the Summerwood Group.

Chapter 12

Health Care and
Human Services

Top 100 Keywords

Acute Care Facility

Adult Services

Advocacy

Ambulatory Care

Anesthesiology

Assisted Living

Behavior Modification

Behavioral Management

Capital Giving Campaign

Cardiology

Case Management

Certificate of Need (CON)

Chemical Dependency

Chronic Care

Clinical Services

Community Hospital

Community Outreach

Continuity of Care

Counseling

Crisis Intervention

Diagnostic Evaluation

Discharge Planning

Dual Diagnosis

Educational Counseling

Electronic Claims Processing

Emergency Medical
   Systems (EMS)

Employee Assistance
   Program (EAP)

Endocrinology

Family Practice

Family Training & Education

Fee Billing

Gastroenterology

Geriatric Medicine

Grant Administration

Group Counseling

Gynecology & Obstetrics

Health Care Administration

Health Care Delivery Systems

Health Maintenance Organization
   (HMO)

Hematology

Holistic Care

Home Health Care

Hospice

Hospital Foundation

Human Services

Independent Life Skills

Industrial Medicine

Infectious Diseases

Inpatient Care

Insurance

Integrated Services Delivery

Intervention

Long-Term Care

Managed Care

Management Service
  Organization (MSO)

Medical

Multi-Hospital Network

Neurology

Occupational Health

Oncology

Ophthalmology

Orthopedics

Outpatient Care

Pathology

Patient Accounting

Patient Care

Patient Education

Pediatrics

Peer Review

Physician Credentialing

Physician Relations

Practice Management

Preferred Provider Organization
  (PPO)

Preventive Medicine

Primary Care

Program Development

Protective Services

Provider Relations

Psychiatry

Psychology

Public Health Administration

Quality of Care

Regulatory Standards

Rehabilitation

Reimbursement

Research

Risk Management

School Counseling

Service Delivery

Social Services

Skilled Nursing Facility

Substance Abuse

Surgery

Testing

Third-Party Administrator

Treatment Planning

Utilization Review

Vital Signs

Vocational Rehabilitation

Wellness Programs

Maria Silvia, BSN

617-893-5130
mariasilvia@yahoo.com

PROFESSIONAL PROFILE

Multilingual new graduate seeking to develop a career as a caring nurse focused on patient safety and best practices for effective patient treatment. Passionate patient advocate who is able to set priorities and effectively organize workload. Demonstrated ability to provide high-quality holistic care to patients and families on a daily basis.

Fluent in English, Portuguese, and Spanish. Proficient in MS Word, Meditech, and patient management databases.

EDUCATION

Bachelor of Science in Nursing, *magna cum laude* • GPA 3.7   May 2016
University of Massachusetts   Boston, MA

Pre-Nursing (12 courses) • Dean's Honor List • GPA 4.0   2011–2013
Bunker Hill Community College   Charlestown, MA

Bachelor of Arts, Languages (Spanish & English), *with honors* • GPA 3.8   2008
University of Coimbra   Coimbra, Portugal

CLINICAL NURSING EXPERIENCE

Clinical Specialty Training Experience		**360 hours**
Chelsea Health Center	Public Health Nursing	90 hours
Boston Children's Hospital	Medical-Surgical Unit/NICU/ICU	67.5 hours
Partners Healthcare	Nursing Education/Sepsis Project	90 hours
Boston Medical Center	L&D/NICU/Antepartum/Postpartum	67.5 hours
Boston Medical Center	Adult & Adolescent Behavioral Health	45 hours
Medical Surgical Nursing		**585 hours**
Beth Israel Deaconess Hospital	Medical-Surgical Unit	180 hours
VA Boston Healthcare System	Medical-Surgical/Hospice Unit	45 hours
Boston Medical Center	ER/OR/ICU/Medical-Surgical/Oncology Units	360 hours

HEALTHCARE-RELATED VOLUNTEER EXPERIENCE

Dana-Farber Cancer Institute • Completed 100+ hours of service, assisting patients and families.	2014–2016
Flu Clinic at Chelsea Health Center • Vaccinated underserved children, adults, and the elderly.	2014
Education Health Fair at UMass Boston • Assisted employees and visitors.	2014
Boston Health Festival • Performed health screening and assisted visitors.	2013

CERTIFICATES/AFFILIATIONS

ACLS Provider	Expires 12/2016
Basic Life Support (BLS/CPR) Provider	Expires 10/2016
Bloodborne Pathogens Training	Completed 07/2014
EKG and Pharmacology Course	Completed 05/1014
HIPPA Privacy and Security Training	Completed 05/2013
Hospital Fire and Life Safety	Expires 05/2017
Mandated Reporter General Training	Completed 09/2014
Member of Sigma Theta Tau International Honor Society of Nursing	Since 10/2014

LESLIE R. SILVERMAN
Altoona, PA 19890
441-388-8273
lessilver@mindspring.com

April 5, 2016

Don Atwood
Director
Hancock Center for Social Services
19 Elm Street
Tucson, AZ 85711

Dear Mr. Atwood:

Eric Green of SPSA Systems suggested that I reach out to you regarding the position of Director—Youth Residential Services for your new residential care and treatment program. Eric is very familiar with the work I have done at Clearwater Rehab Consultants, in Pennsylvania, and knows that I am seeking a move back to the Southwest for family reasons.

Recruited to Clearwater in 2012, I was challenged to build and manage a residential rehabilitation program for chronic youth offenders, most of whom were diagnosed with a combination of psychological, behavioral, and emotional problems. Since our beginning, my team and I have serviced more than 2000 youth offenders.

Most remarkably, our recidivism rate is less than 10%, clearly demonstrating the effectiveness of both our residential and follow-up programs.

I am quite interested in learning more about your soon-to-open facility and explore how my experience can be of value. I will phone your office next week to arrange a meeting at a mutually agreeable time. Thank you in advance.

Sincerely,

Leslie R. Silverman

Keyword Answers to Interview Questions

Tell me about yourself.

First and foremost, I'm a physician with more than 15 years' experience in the delivery of patient care, working primarily in the medical disciplines of neurology and neurophysiology.

Just as significant, I am an experienced hospital administrator with current responsibility for the profitable management of a 234-bed acute care hospital in Boston. My responsibilities range from the daily operations of the hospital and all patient care programs to a host of administrative, regulatory, and financial affairs. I am currently working on a Certificate of Need application for $35 million to fund development of a new rehab facility and several community outreach programs to enhance the public's use of our hospital.

I enjoy the challenge of using both medical and managerial skills to create health care systems that work for our patients, staff, and community.

What is the most valuable skill you bring to our company?

The fact that I am both a doctor and an administrator is my greatest strength. I manage from both a hands-on health care delivery perspective as well as that of a manager, concerned with dollars, resources, personnel, and facilities. The interrelationship of the two is what has been at the foundation of my entire career success.

What is your most significant achievement?

As a physician, my greatest achievement is the positive impact I've made in the lives of hundreds of patients, many of whom had resigned themselves to living with chronic neurological conditions. Through the tremendous advances in the field of neurology, I've been able to give them back quality of life and time.

I've also been a pioneer in the managed care arena, working with insurance companies, providers, and health care facilities to create programs responsive to our community's needs.

A great example is the recent effort I led to launch a "healthy choices" clinic in one of Boston's poorest neighborhoods. I gained support from health insurers and came up with an innovative staffing solution that allowed hospital workers to add shifts at the new facility without losing their primary position. We now offer a wide range of services to help residents of an underserved neighborhood make wise lifestyle and health choices.

Chapter 13

Hospitality and Food Service

Top 100 Keywords

Amenities

Automated Check-In/Out

Back-of-the-House Operations

Banquets

Budget Administration

Building Maintenance

Capacity Planning

Catering

Club Management

Concierge Services

Conferences

Contract Negotiation &
   Administration

Conventions

Corporate Dining Room

Corporate Events

Cost Control

Country Club

Customer Retention

Customer Service & Satisfaction

Dining Room

Emergency Evacuation

Engineering Maintenance

Event Orders

Expeditions

Expense Control

Facilities Engineering

Fast-Food Establishment

Financial Analysis & Reporting

Fine Dining

Food & Beverage (F&B)

Food Cost Controls

Food Preparation

Food Service

Front Desk

Front-of-the-House Operations

Guest Registration

Guest Relations

Guest Retention

Guest Satisfaction

Hospitality

Hotel Management

Hotel Operations

Housekeeping

Human Resources

Inventory Planning & Control

Kitchen Operations

Kitchenware

Labor Cost Control

Lodging

Logistics

Maintenance & Repair

Marketing

Meeting Planning

Member Development

Member Retention

Menu Planning

Menu Pricing

Motel

Multi-Site Operations

Occupancy

Point-of-Sale (POS) Systems

Portion Control

Private Club

Property Development

Property Management

Publicity

Purchasing

Recreational Facilities

Registration Services

Reservations

Resort

Restaurant Management

Restaurant Operations

Revenue Per Available Room (REVPAR)

Room Rates

Room Service

Rooms Revenue

Sales

Security

Service

Signature Property

Sleeping Rooms

Social Media

Spa Operations

Special Events

Staffing

Supply Management

Team Building

Technology

Telecommunications

Tourism

Tourist Attractions

Training & Development

Transportation

Travel

Travel Agency

Union Labor

Valet Services

Vendors

VIP Relations

Rene Balzac, CHA

847-437-8621   Chicago, IL 60616   renebalzac@gmail.com

HOSPITALITY MANAGER
Lester, Sunrise & Hyatt Hotels Experience

Consistently successful in increasing revenues, guest service/satisfaction, and profitability.

- Sales & Marketing Management
- Award-Winning Customer Service
- Food & Beverage Operations
- Human Resources Affairs

- Finance & Budget Administration
- Project Management
- Marketing Pricing & Analysis
- New Product & Service Development

Certified Hotel Administrator
Fluent English, French (mother tongue), and Spanish. Conversational German.

PROFESSIONAL EXPERIENCE

HOTEL LESTER, Chicago, IL   2014–2016

Resident Manager
5-star Relais & Chateaux property • 68 full-service suites • full F&B, including renowned fine-dining restaurant

Held full P&L responsibility for one of the most exclusive properties in Chicago. Directed the entire operation—all financial affairs, facilities management, and F&B—and team of 150+.

- Increased restaurant revenue 40% and banquet sales 33% via comprehensive marketing and advertising campaign emphasizing quality, service, and uniqueness.
- Led guest services team to "Lester Luster" award recognizing "diamond-level" service standard.

SUNRISE HOTELS INTERNATIONAL   2009–2014

Special Projects Manager, Chicago, IL (2011–2014)

Managed a diversity of corporate assignments involving new property development, property acquisition/feasibility analysis, and property turnaround/reorganization. Supervised financial analysis, prepared cash flow projections and debt service pro-formas, and provided financial support for potential acquisitions in FL, NY, and IA.

- Directed a complete renovation and re-opening of the Sunrise Hotel in Boca Raton.
- Wrote corporate operations manual for affiliated hotels and restaurants.

Assistant Manager, Sunrise Hotel, Chicago, IL (2009–2011)
3-star, 368-room, 220-employee hotel • F&B for 2 restaurants, 1 bar, 7 banquet rooms, 24-hour room service

Worked closely with hotel manager in directing human resources, labor relations, training, purchasing, budgeting, guest relations, security, facilities, and daily business operations. Personally managed sales, marketing, and business development campaigns.

- Contributed to 135% revenue growth (to $9.5M) and 700% surge in gross operating profit (to $3.5M).
- Directed $4.5M renovation of the TowerSuite (12 units) and 4 banquet rooms.

HYATT INTERNATIONAL   2005–2009

Area Operations Analyst, Caribbean-Central America (2008–2009)

Conducted operational, profit, quality, and performance reviews of the 7 Hyatt properties in the Caribbean-Central American Region. Worked cooperatively with on-site management teams to facilitate operational improvements.

Hotel Operations Analyst, Caracas Hyatt, Caracas, Venezuela (2006–2008)
Purchasing Director / F&B Controller, Bogota Hyatt, Bogota, Colombia (2005–2006)

EDUCATION

Diploma—Ecole Hoteliere S.S.H., Lausanne, Switzerland
Diploma—Business Management, Lausanne, Switzerland

Thomas Washington
425 Armadillo Avenue
Rosemont, TX 77877
299-432-3927 • tom.washington@yahoo.com

March 5, 2016

Paul Kirwin
President—Country Inns & Suites
Country Hospitality Worldwide
P.O. Box 59159
Minneapolis, MN 55459-8203

Dear Mr. Kirwin:

Congratulations! I've been watching the development of your new property in Rosemont, Texas, and can tell you that the entire community is looking forward to the grand opening. We've needed a property of this type in Rosemont for several years (as I'm sure your demographics indicated), and I know that the project will be extremely profitable if well led.

I'm a resident of Rosemont with a wealth of business experience worldwide. Having recently returned to live permanently in the area, I would welcome the opportunity to interview with you or a member of your staff for a management position with your new property. Let me tell you why I am the "perfect" candidate (albeit atypical):

- 15+ years of general management experience in facilities development and management, including planning, budgeting, logistics, purchasing, equipment, materials, and technology.

- Outstanding communication and people-to-people interaction skills. I am well known throughout the local market, have extensive contacts in both the professional and civic communities, and recently completed a yearlong leadership training course with the City.

- Ability to "get the job done" no matter the circumstance. This was critical throughout my career, often working in environments with stringent deadlines and financial expectations.

- Strong qualifications in training, development, and leadership, with direct responsibility for hundreds of employees, supervisors, and managers and multimillion-dollar budgets.

- In-depth understanding of customer service, customer loyalty, and customer retention.

I would like to share with you some ideas I have for launching Rosemont with a "bang"—ideas that will resonate in the local community and create positive goodwill that will benefit your hotel for years to come. I will follow up with a phone call next week—I look forward to speaking with you!

Sincerely,

Thomas Washington

Keyword Answers to Interview Questions

Tell me about yourself.

When I arrived on-site at the Meridien Hotel, there was an empty building. It was lovely, brand new, and on beautiful grounds. But there was nothing inside— no employees, no guests, no F&B, no front desk, no housekeeping ... nothing.

The owner said, "Here's your hotel and three administrative people to help you. Can you have the hotel up and running within two months?" Well, long story short, we did it. Two months to the day after I arrived, we held our grand opening to a huge audience and 100% capacity the first night!

So, if you ask me about myself, it's that I'm the "hotel start-up guy," able to quickly, cost-effectively, and efficiently launch new properties to rave reviews, strong financial performance, and a keen commitment to the finest in guest services.

What is the most valuable skill you bring to our company?

Undeniably, my best skills are my abilities to organize and prioritize. Whether I'm opening a new hotel, introducing a new PC-based reservations management system, or designing guest amenities, I have consistently delivered projects on time and within budget because of my ability to plan, organize, prioritize, and execute.

This is the value and strength I bring to all of my operations and my special projects, and is what I will deliver to you and your stockholders.

What is your most significant achievement?

My greatest achievement is the opening of the Meridien Hotel in just two months. This was a 249-room resort property with complete spa facilities, three F&B outlets, and 18 acres of grounds and landscaping. Starting with nothing, I opened a hotel 60 days later with a staff of 72. We were truly amazed.

During that time, I did everything ... budgeting, hiring, training, management development, menu planning and pricing, purchasing, security, and most significantly, marketing. In fact, by opening day we had more than $500,000 in business meeting commitments for the first 30 days.

Chapter 14

Human Resources

Top 100 Keywords

Americans with Disabilities
    Act (ADA)

Arbitration

Benefits Administration

Career Coaching

Career Development

Career Planning & Management

Career Track

Change Management

Claims Administration

Collective Bargaining

College Recruitment

Compensation

Competency-Based Performance

Contingent Recruitment

Contract Employment

Corporate Culture Change

Cross-Cultural Communications

Culture Change

Diversity

Downsizing

Electronic Applicant Screening

Employee Assistance Program
    (EAP)

Employee Benefits

Employee Communications

Employee Relations

Employee Retention

Employee Surveys

Employment Contracts

Equal Employment Opportunity
    (EEO)

Executive Coaching

Executive Recruitment

Exempt & Non-Exempt
    Personnel

Expatriate Employment

Family Medical Leave Act (FMLA)

Grievance Proceedings

Human Capital

Human Resources (HR)

Human Resources Generalist
    Affairs

Human Resources Information
    Systems (HRIS)

Incentive Planning

Insurance

International Employment

Job Task Analysis

Labor Contract Negotiations

Labor Laws

Labor Relations

Leadership Assessment

Leadership Development

Management Training & Development

Manpower Planning

Matrix Management

Morale & Welfare

Multimedia Training & Instruction

Multinational Workforce

Occupation

Occupational Analysis

Occupational Classification

Online Recruitment

Organization(al) Design

Organization(al) Development (OD)

Organization(al) Needs Assessment

Participative Management

Pay-for-Performance

Pension Administration

Performance Appraisal

Performance Incentives

Performance Reengineering

Personnel Management

Personnel Relations

Policies & Procedures

Position Classification

Process Improvement

Profit-Sharing Plan

Promotions

Recordkeeping

Recruitment

Regulatory Affairs

Regulatory Compliance & Reporting

Retention

Safety Training

Salary Administration

Self-Directed Work Teams

Social Media Recruitment

Staffing

Succession Planning

Talent Management

Task Analysis

Team Building & Leadership

Technology

Termination

Train-the-Trainer

Training & Development

Union-Management Negotiations

Union Negotiations

Union Relations

Wage & Salary Administration

Wellness Program

Workforce

Workforce Reengineering

Workplace Safety

Patricia Hightower

Washington, DC 22302 — 202-252-2300 — patricia.hightower@gmail.com — LinkedIn.com/in/patriciahightower

HUMAN RESOURCES PROFESSIONAL

▶ **Generalist HR Affairs** for organizations as large as 700 employees—US and international locations.

▶ **Learning & Development,** launching programs to build high-performance workforce and develop future leaders.

▶ **Change Management** for HR initiatives, organizational reengineering efforts, and strategic corporate transformations.

PROFESSIONAL EXPERIENCE

PINEVIEW LTD., Washington, DC—2013–Present

Senior Director—Human Resources—Change management and HR leadership for $125M company with 550 employees and 7 operating locations in US and Finland.

Challenge	Lead HR from a traditional labor relations function to an integrated, comprehensive HR organization with a focus on leadership development, best-in-class HR programs, and tactical support for strategic business operations and financial objectives.
Actions & Results	▶ Introduced metrics-based performance management system that instilled results focus company-wide. Implemented employee recognition and awards programs.
	▶ Created learning and development committee to gain input from all business units and launched leadership, cultural awareness, and teambuilding concepts and programs.
	▶ Captured $200K in benefit cost reductions and avoided additional $1.2M in SERP funding.
	▶ Championed successful EH&S program design, implementation, and company-wide employee communications and training initiative.
	▶ Realigned senior management compensation programs, created format for gainsharing, introduced mid-management incentives, tied variable compensation to business plans, and initiated modified Hay evaluation instrument for pharmaceutical business unit.

AIR SYSTEMS, INC., Chester, PA—2005–2013

Human Resources Manager—Chemicals (2010–2013)—HR generalist affairs—recruitment, staffing, training, compensation, benefits, employee relations, succession planning—for $500M division with 700 employees in 120 locations.

Challenge	Introduce improved HR strategies, services, and programs into the company's largest division.
Actions & Results	▶ Spearheaded division-wide HR planning, job realignment, employee involvement, teambuilding, and organization development projects.
	▶ Directed major plant divestiture and re-employment of all 125 employees.
	▶ Realigned and strengthened compensation programs and salary administration.
	▶ Taught Zenger Miller Frontline Leadership and Crosby Quality programs.

Plant Human Resources Manager (2008–2010) for company's largest chemical manufacturing facility. Complete generalist and labor relations responsibilities.

Human Resources Associate (2005–2008) involved with recruitment, benefits administration, and labor negotiations for 500+ employees at 5 manufacturing sites.

EDUCATION

INDIANA UNIVERSITY—**BS Business Management** (2005)
HARVARD BUSINESS SCHOOL—**Strategic Human Resources Management**
UNIVERSITY OF MICHIGAN—**Labor Relations Management**

Robert McKinney
617-345-0511
robert.mckinney@gmail.com

May 17, 2016

Janice Lawrence
VP Human Resources
Calipari Enterprises
Reading, MA 01867

Dear Ms. Lawrence:

Susan Shanley suggested that I get in touch with you regarding your current opening for a **Human Resources Generalist**.

An HR professional with strong qualifications in all core generalist functions, I have been instrumental in strengthening company performance through my efforts in:

- Recruitment & Staffing
- Learning & Development
- Benefits Management & Cost Reduction
- HRIS Technology
- Employee Relations
- Regulatory Compliance

In the past 5 years with Seatex Pharma, I led diverse recruiting efforts as we sought to add scientific and technical personnel in an extremely competitive hiring climate. One of my most effective strategies was to launch "meet and greet" Thursday nights at our downtown headquarters. We built relationships with prospective employees, extended our network, and established Seatex as a great place to work.

The result? More than 50% of our new hires come from referrals, and they have proven to be among our most valuable employees.

As you may know, Seatex is relocating to the South Shore, and I have decided to look for a new position closer to my home in Andover. Susan has told me great things about Calipari, and I am very interested to learn if there is fit between your needs and my expertise. I will follow up with a phone call on Friday and hope that we can meet soon. Thank you.

Sincerely,

Robert McKinney

Enclosure: Resume

Keyword Answers to Interview Questions

Tell me about yourself.

I'm an HR generalist with nine years' experience in all core HR functions … interviewing, hiring, job placement, employee relations, compensation, benefits, employee recognition, and training and development.

My greatest successes, however, have been in workforce downsizing which, unfortunately, I know is one of your greatest needs. First with IBM and then with Bank of America, I've orchestrated the layoff of more than 3,000 employees over the past five years. It certainly is not a very pleasant experience, but it's a reality of business today and a reality that I'm particularly adept at managing.

One of my innovations was creating in-house outplacement programs that provide employees with the tools and resources that they need to manage successful job searches and find new employment. By adding a real human touch, everyone has benefited. And, not only were these programs more cost-effective than using outside firms, they produced much better results.

What is the most valuable skill you bring to our company?

My ability to build rapport is what I consider to be my most significant attribute. I have excellent interpersonal relationship and communication skills and am comfortable in virtually every situation—from the board room to the manufacturing floor.

What's more, I have a real appreciation for each and every employee, realizing that any business is only as strong as the commitment of its workforce. As an HR professional, it is my job to make those employees feel valued through their individual contributions.

What is your most significant achievement?

I've previously addressed my accomplishments in workforce downsizing, so let me focus here on my success in training and development. One of the greatest advantages to working with a company the size of Bank of America is the diversity of the workforce and, in turn, the diversity of training I developed.

One month I'd be working on designing a program to train new members of the call-center team; the next month I'd be creating a leadership training program for the senior management team. In total, I designed and delivered more than 30 different programs to more than 2,000 employees.

Chapter 15

Information Technology

Top 100 Keywords

Agile Development

Application Development

Architecture

Artificial Intelligence (AI)

Benchmarking

Big Data

Business Continuity

Business Intelligence (BI)

Capacity Planning

Capital Budgets

Client Server Architecture

Cloud Solutions

Computer Science

Content Development

Data Center Operations

Data Mining & Warehousing

Data Recovery

Database Administration

Database Design & Development

Database Integration

Digital Media

Digital Technology

Disaster Recovery

E-Commerce

Electronic Data Interchange (EDI)

Emerging Technologies

Enterprise Architecture

Enterprise Systems

Geographic Information System
    (GIS)

Global Resource Management

Global Systems Support

Graphical User Interface (GUI)

Hardware Configuration

Hardware Development &
    Engineering

Help Desk

Imaging Technology

Information Security

Information Systems (IS)

Information Technology (IT)

Infrastructure

Infrastructure as a Service (IaaS)

Internet

Internet of Things (IoT)

Intranet

IT Governance

IT Shared Services

ITIL / IT Service Management (ITSM)

Knowledge Management

Licensing

Local Area Network (LAN)

Multi-Platform Integration

Multimedia Technology

Needs Assessment

Network Administration

Network Protocol

New Media

Next-Generation Technology

Online

Operating System

Operations Support Systems (OSS)

Pilot Implementation

Platform as a Service (PaaS)

Process Reengineering

Program Management

Programming

Project Lifecycle

Project Management

Project Methodology

Quality Assurance (QA)

Real-Time Data

Relational Database

Research & Development (R&D)

Resource Management

Root Cause Analysis

Scalability

Social Media

Software as a Service (SaaS)

Software Configuration

Software Development & Engineering

Software Solutions

Solutions Development & Delivery

Systems Administration

Systems Configuration

Systems Documentation

Systems Engineering

Systems Integration

Technical Documentation

Technical Training & Support

Technology Commercialization

Technology Integration

Technology Needs Assessment

Technology Solutions

Technology Transfer

User Support

Vendor Management

Virtualization

Web Administration   Websites

Web-Based Technology   Wide Area Network (WAN)

NOTE: It is essential that you include your SPECIFIC technology skills (hardware, software, network protocols, programming languages, etc.) in your resume, along with all of the relevant keywords from the list on the previous pages.

You can include those tech skills in the summary section of your resume, in a separate section titled "Technology Skills," "Technology Qualifications," or "Technology Profile," or you can integrate them into your job descriptions. Without them, your resume will most likely be passed over by electronic keyword scanning systems (also known as ATS technology), so be certain to prominently display them.

Keisha Jones

818-678-5555

http://www.LinkedIn.com/keishajones

keishajones@gmail.com

Web Developer / System Administrator

Operating Systems	Solaris—UNIX—Windows
Server Systems	Windows Server 2012—Apache—MS Exchange—IIS—VMware—Hypervisor
Programing Languages	JavaScript—ColdFusion—HTML—Perl
Software	Office365—MS Office—MS Outlook—MS Access—Adobe Photoshop

EXPERIENCE   U. S. Army   2010–Present

Web Developer
- Direct 9 web programmers who administer, operate, and maintain a $4M intranet and database system.
- Provide oversight of 300K documents (28 gigabytes of disk space) on the web server. Directly maintain more than 25K files, including all ColdFusion files.

- Cut systems maintenance and support costs 66% (saving $55K per year) and increased speed of service 38% by consolidating multiple web servers.
- Planned and consolidated cutting-edge intranet environment during the first phase of a Unix-to-Windows transition effort.
- Created search capability for more than 1000 forms and publications on the web server, saving time and effort in locating data. Awarded the **Quality Leadership Team Award** for this implementation.

Systems Administrator
- Install new end-user systems, platforms, associated file servers, and application software.
- Serve as Systems Security Officer for a worldwide network.
- Supervise 7 computer programmers who maintain all automation requirements.
- Manage 11 technicians supporting 800+ workstations, LANs, and worldwide networks.
- Control and maintain $1M+ in computer parts and equipment and an annual budget above $300K.

- Selected from many as a member of the LAN install team, which implemented more than 400 LAN accounts during a 3-month period.
- Designed and developed programs to improve system security and efficiency. Rewrote the software utilized to grant and revalidate user access to the host computer system.

EDUCATION & TRAINING

BS Computer Science, University of Rhode Island, North Kingstown, RI   2015
AA Liberal Arts, Rhode Island College, Warwick, RI   2008

Project Management	2015	MS Project	2012
Project Budgeting & Administration	2014	Internetworking with TCP/IP	2010
Web Site Fundamentals	2013	Supporting MS Windows NT Server	2009
Web Security and Administration	2013	Solaris	2009
JavaScript Fundamentals	2012	Advanced PC Troubleshooting	2009

RHONDA SHIPLEY

rhonda.shipley@gmail.com • 312-611-9004

March 15, 2016

Elizabeth Hawkins
Vice President of Administration
Children's Hospital Boston
300 Longwood Avenue
Boston, MA 02115

Dear Ms. Hawkins:

Steve Adams suggested that I contact you as the first step in exploring career opportunities with Children's Hospital. I would certainly appreciate any suggestions you might have as well as a referral to the appropriate person within the Information Technology Department at Children's.

I am an experienced IT manager who can visualize, strategize, plan, and deliver technology solutions that support operating goals. Throughout my career, I have delivered exceptional services and innovations within organizations that have unusual and rigorous challenges that seem to parallel the environment at Children's:

- rapid, multi-site growth
- high volume of users
- multiple stakeholders
- intense regulatory and data security demands
- high-stakes projects with rigid deadlines
- rapid, often disruptive technological advances

I am impressed with what I have been reading about the forward-thinking technology environment at Children's, and I'd like to bring my broad skill-set and diverse experiences to such a dynamic organization. After five years in Chicago, my spouse and I are planning a move back to the Boston area. In fact, I will be in the city at the end of next month and could easily schedule a meeting with you or another appropriate person at Children's.

I will follow up with a phone call on Wednesday to see what advice and suggestions you might have. In advance, thank you for your assistance.

Sincerely,

Rhonda Shipley

Keyword Answers to Interview Questions

Tell me about yourself.

I am a software designer and engineer, successful in taking projects from theoretical concept through technical design and prototype development to final market launch. Beginning my career with Nokia in 2000, I was involved in the initial technical, functional, and applications design of Nokia's global supply chain management platform.

Recruited to GRX in 2005, I continued with the development of new supply chain and logistics systems. Today GRX is recognized for having the best logistics technology solutions in the world. In total, I've participated in and/or led more than 20 new software development programs for products now generating combined annual revenues of $20 million to GRX.

What is the most valuable skill you bring to our company?

My most valuable skill is my ability to fast-track projects. In fact, 16 of the 20 projects I've been involved in during my tenure with GRX have been delivered ahead of schedule and at a minimum of $50,000 under budget.

Not only do I consider this to be my strongest skill, so does GRX! They've honored me with numerous corporate awards for my technical, project management, and financial contributions to the company.

What is your most significant achievement?

Without a doubt, my most notable accomplishment has been the cost savings I've produced for GRX. As I mentioned previously, I've delivered several projects well under budget for a total cost savings of more than $1.2 million over the past 5 years.

When you consider the time, expense, personnel, and technology resources involved in developing new software, this has been a remarkable achievement in a time of over-inflated prices, challenging economic conditions, and intense competition.

Chapter 16

Law, Legal Affairs, and Law Enforcement

Top 100 Keywords

Acquisition

Adjudication

Administrative Law

Antitrust

Appeal

Arbitration

Background Investigation

Briefs

Business Law

Case Law

Case Management

Chapter 7 Bankruptcy

Chapter 11 Bankruptcy

Client Management

Competitive Intelligence

Constitutional Law

Contracts Law

Copyright Law

Corporate By-Laws

Corporate Legal Affairs

Corporate Recordkeeping

Corporate Security

Court Rulings

Courtroom Proceedings

Criminal Investigation

Criminal Justice

Criminal Law

Crisis Response

Cross-Border Transactions

Deposition

Defense

Discovery

Due Diligence

Employment Law

Environmental Law

Ethics

Evidence

Executive Protection

Family Law

Federal Jurisdiction

Felony

Fraud

Government Rules & Regulations

Intellectual Property

Interrogation

Investigation

Joint Venture

Judicial Affairs

Jurisprudence

Jury

Labor Arbitration

Labor Law

Landmark Decision

Law

Law Enforcement

Law Review

Legal Advocacy

Legal Affairs

Legal Research & Reporting

Legal Transactions

Legislative Review & Analysis

Liability

Licensing

Limited Liability Corporation (LLC)

Limited Partnership

Litigation

Mediation

Medical Malpractice

Memoranda

Mergers

Motions

Negotiations

Patent Law

Personal Injury

Pleadings

Precedent

Private Investigation

Probate Law

Prosecution

Public Records

Public Safety

Real Estate Law

Risk Management

Security

Settlement Negotiations

Shareholder Relations

Signatory Authority

State Jurisdiction

Strategic Alliance

Tax Law

Technology Transfer

Testimony

Trade Secrets

Trademark

Transactions Law

Trial Proceedings

Video Surveillance

VIP Protection

Weapons Screening

Witness Protection

ELIZABETH PARKER

415-493-7459 | elizabethparker@mac.com
LinkedIn.com/in/ElizabethParker

CORPORATE COUNSEL

Technology Licensing | Mergers & Acquisitions | Joint Ventures | Patents & Trademarks
Litigation & Claims Defense | Corporate Finance | Human Resource Affairs | Contracts

PROFESSIONAL EXPERIENCE

PFIZER, INC., Redwood Valley, CA

Associate General Counsel & Corporate Secretary   2014–Present

Recruited back to previous employer as Senior Counsel responsible for worldwide intellectual property (IP) affairs and licensing, with an IP portfolio of 7500+ trademarks and 1500 patents. Direct a staff of 11, including 5 attorneys and 3 paralegals. Manage $5M operating budget.

- Structure and negotiate licensing contracts with global pharmaceutical companies, biotechnology firms, and universities for product acquisitions. Negotiate co-promotion, distribution, and supply agreements worldwide.

- Direct all patent and trademark origination, enforcement, and defense actions worldwide. Travel throughout Europe, Japan, Australia, and North America.

- Provide legal consultation for merger, acquisition, and joint venture transactions. Select and direct outside counsel worldwide.

NOTABLE: Accelerated number of patent awards through improved legal process. Ranked by Intellectual Property Office as one of the top 200 organizations worldwide in number of US patents granted in 2015.

MERIWETHER RESEARCH & DEVELOPMENT COMPANY, San Jose, CA

General Counsel, CFO & Secretary   2010–2014

Hired to direct drug development company's IPO following its spin-off from Allergan Pharmaceuticals. Raised $25M and placed stock on NASDAQ (managed by Merrill Lynch). Achieved market capitalization of $250M.

- Held full accountability for all IP, general and corporate legal, financial, accounting, and human resource affairs for the corporation. Directed a staff of 15.

- Managed a large out-licensing effort for drug development candidates and adjuncts, corporate financial and strategic planning, budgeting, contracts, JVs, and long-range corporate development functions.

NOTABLE: Patented and licensed CLEOCIN-T, FDA-approved prescription antibiotic acne formulation that delivered $50M+ in annual revenues. Raised additional $5M in revenues through negotiation of strategic R&D partnerships with major multinational and regional pharmaceutical companies in Japan and Europe.

ELIZABETH PARKER

415-493-7459 | elizabethparker@mac.com | Page 2

PFIZER , INC., Irvine, CA

Assistant General Counsel—Allergan International Division   2005–2010

- Legal Counsel directing Allergan's IP, corporate development, contracts, in-licensing and out-licensing programs worldwide.

NOTABLE: Spearheaded the start-up of new company subsidiaries, manufacturing operations, and joint ventures in the UK, France, Italy, Japan, and Ireland.

Associate Counsel—Nelson Research Division   2000–2005

- Participated in corporate development, merger, acquisition, licensing, contracts, and drug development programs worldwide.

- Guided top scientists in early-stage development of computer-assisted drug design technologies.

NOTABLE: Directed the award of 50+ patents with numerous foreign corresponding patents and licenses.

EDUCATION

JD (Honors), The George Washington University National Law Center
MBA, Pepperdine University School of Business and Management
BS (Chemistry), University of California at Berkeley

PROFESSIONAL ACTIVITIES

Bar Admissions   State Bar of California | US Patent and Trademark Office Bar | US Supreme Court

Associations   American Intellectual Property Law Association
Licensing Executives Society
American Corporate Patent Counsel, Editorial Board (Managing Intellectual Property)

Publications   Editorial Board Member & Contributing Writer to "Managing Intellectual Property," European-based monthly legal publication:
— *"Patent Practitioners—Don't Let GATT Get You,"* March 2014 (republished by IP section of California State Bar)
— *"Intellectual Property and Pharmaceuticals,"* Patent Yearbook, 2012

Presentations   Presentations sponsored by the Practicing Law Institute (PLI) in San Francisco, published by PLI in its "Global Intellectual Property Series":
— *"Patent Litigation in Civil Law Countries,"* 2015
— *"Contact Lens Care Litigation,"* 2014

Reynolds Arrington

Fayetteville, NC 27066
teynolds.arrington@aol.com
919-637-0815

June 1, 2016

Lucy Markman
Director of Security Operations
TXD Security Systems & Technologies, Inc.
11 Main Boulevard, Suite 1190
Dallas, TX 78900

Dear Ms. Markman:

As the **Facilities Security Manager** for Dixie Metric Materials in Fayetteville, NC, I have been one of the driving forces in the creation of a comprehensive, plant-wide security program. With a staff of only 12, we have implemented systems to protect both our physical assets and our intellectual property.

Most impressive, we have accomplished all of this—electronic surveillance, emergency preparedness and response, Internet security, personnel security—in just three short years.

Prior to my career with Dixie, I served with the NYC Police Department for 12 years, first as a patrol officer and later as a detective in the Terrorism Prevention Division. As such, you can see that my experience is extremely relevant to your search for a **Manager of Facilities Security & Emergency Response**.

Aware of the quality of your organization and its personnel, I would be delighted to have the opportunity for a personal interview. I am traveling this week to coordinate several security tech systems upgrades but will be back in my office at the end of next week and will follow up with you then.

I appreciate your consideration and can guarantee that the depth and scope of my experience will add measurable value and safety to your company, its facilities, and your personnel. Thank you.

Sincerely,

Reynolds Arrington

Enclosure

Keyword Answers to Interview Questions

Tell me about yourself.

I am a corporate attorney with a wealth of experience in corporate law and litigation, intellectual property, technology licensing, copyright law, contract law, and international trade.

Following graduation from Temple University School of Law, I began my legal career as an Associate with Marsh & McClennan. Within two years, I was recruited to McAlister, Banner & Smith, where I started to specialize in the technology industry and related corporate legal affairs.

During my tenure with McAlister, I negotiated some of the first-ever technology transfer agreements on behalf of TechStars. My relationship with TechStars was so strong that they actively recruited me for more than a year until I accepted my current position as corporate counsel for the $2.8 billion technology division. In this capacity, I orchestrate all corporate legal affairs for operations in 62 countries worldwide with a total workforce of more than 50,000.

What is the most valuable skill you bring to our company?

My negotiating skills are, by far, my strongest skill. Couple that with my ability to quickly build rapport with other attorneys, bankers, financiers, venture capitalists, corporate executives, and regulators, and you have uncovered the basis for my career success.

Despite often conflicting agendas, tight financial constraints, and critical concerns about protecting proprietary information and technology, I have been able to negotiate large-dollar contracts to the benefit of all involved parties. In fact, based on my expertise, I have often been personally selected by TechStars' Board of Directors to handle the company's most complex and most sensitive negotiations.

What is your most significant achievement?

During TechStars' 2012 expansion into India, I personally negotiated contracts with both government officials and the management team at the helm of India's entire telecommunications infrastructure.

This was an unbelievably challenging negotiation involving more than 55 people, 8 companies, and 16 government agencies. TechStars received all regulatory approvals within a record-breaking 120 days, I negotiated several joint ventures, and TechStars is now the market leader.

Chapter 17

Manufacturing and Production Operations

Top 100 Keywords

Assembly Line

Automated Control Systems

Automated Manufacturing

Budget Development & Administration

Capacity Planning

Capital Asset

Capital Project

Cell Manufacturing

Computer-Aided Design (CAD)

Computer-Aided Manufacturing (CAM)

Computer Controls

Computer Engineering

Computer-Integrated Manufacturing (CIM)

Computer Technology

Continuous Improvement

Cost Avoidance & Reduction

Cross-Functional Teams

Cycle Time Reduction

Data Collection & Analysis

Defect Analysis

Distribution Operations

Efficiency Improvement

Electromechanical Engineering

Electronics

Engineering

Environmental Health & Safety (EHS)

Equipment Financing

Equipment Maintenance & Repair

Equipment Operations

Ergonomics

Fabrication

Facilities Management

Factory Operations

Finished Goods

Hazardous Materials (HAZMAT)

Industrial Engineering

Inventory Planning

Inventory Planning & Control

Just-In-Time (JIT)

Labor Efficiency

Labor Relations

Logistics

Manufacturing Engineering

Manufacturing Operations

Manufacturing Technology

Master Schedule

Materials Planning

Materials Replenishment
    System (MRP)

Mechanical Engineering

Metrics & Measurements

Multi-Site Operations

Offshore

On-Time Delivery

Operating Budget

Operations Management

Operations Reengineering

Operations Start-Up

Optimization

Order Processing & Fulfillment

OSHA Regulations

Outsourcing

Performance Improvement

Performance Measurement

Pilot Plant

Plant Operations

Process Automation

Process Design & Reengineering

Process Technology

Procurement

Product Development &
    Engineering

Production Lead Time

Production Management

Production Plans & Schedules

Production Output

Productivity

Profit & Loss (P&L)
    Management

Purchasing

Quality Assurance (QA)

Quality Control

Regulatory Compliance &
    Reporting

Research & Development (R&D)

Safety Management

Safety Training

Shipping & Receiving

Spares & Repairs

Specifications

Statistical Process Control (SPC)

Supplier Management

Supplier Quality

Technology Integration

Time & Motion Studies

Traffic Management

Union Negotiations

Value-Added Processes

Vendor Quality Certification

Warehousing

World-Class Manufacturing

Workflow Optimization

Workforce Management

Yield Improvement

Meredith Rockwell

http://www.linkedin.com/in/meredithrockwell

301-745-7299 • rockwell@yahoo.com
Baltimore, MD 21229

Manufacturing Operations Manager

Building & Leading World-Class Manufacturing & Distribution Organizations
Lean Manufacturing • Six Sigma (Black Belt) • Continuous Process Improvement

Delivered "impossible" performance improvements in demanding industries.

Professional Experience

BIGBOX, INC., Baltimore, MD   2014–Present
Operations Manager / Six Sigma Black Belt

Productivity, safety, and quality for 1M-SF distribution center | 350 employees | Six Sigma project leadership

Achieved first profitability in 6 years of operation by driving continuous performance improvements that slashed operating costs.

- Increased throughput **33%** and order accuracy **44%** via daily planning and a performance-review process.

- Boosted order-picking productivity **12%** by establishing performance expectations and accountability.

- Led 2 Black Belt projects that delivered savings of **$260K**, reduced errors by **50%**, and found a permanent solution for a recurring problem—subsequently applied at 3 national distribution sites.

- Met high-volume delivery goals with **zero** overtime and **52%** improvement in accuracy by developing an innovative learning-curve model for temporary associates during the peak holiday season.

KLEIN AUTO SYSTEMS, Baltimore, MD   2004–2014
Program Group Manager, Climate Systems Division, 2011–2014

P&L, strategic planning, business development, sales, manufacturing engineering, Lean/Six Sigma | $60M, 300-employee division | Production of auto climate-control systems | QS 9000 production environment

Turned around unprofitable business unit via aggressive cost reductions and productivity gains.

- Slashed production costs for existing products; landed new business; reconfigured line from batch to lean continuous flow for greater productivity. Results:

	Sales	Pretax Net Profit	Models	Inventory Turns
2013	$31.8M	23.4%	8	100+
2012	$16.7M	10.4%	4	64
2011	$12.6M	(3.4%)	4	36

- Eradicated #1 cause of expansion-device warranty claims and shaved **10%** off warranty costs.

- Managed downsizing that drove **$2M (15%)** from annual costs without affecting customer satisfaction.

- Secured new programs valued at **$32M,** leading team presentation to the division's largest customer.

- Landed and successfully launched multiple programs for customers such as Daimler-Chrysler, GM, Ford, Peterbilt, Kenworth, International, John Deere, and JCB.

Meredith Rockwell

301-745-7299 • rockwell@yahoo.com

KLEIN AUTO SYSTEMS, continued
Program Manager, Off-Highway Group, 2008–2011

P&L, new business development, manufacturing engineering, customer service, sales forecasting | 7 staff

Restored profitability, expanded market penetration, and diversified product offerings for sustainable growth. Introduced Lean Manufacturing to the Group.

- Added **$1.6M** to the bottom line; improved product throughput **46%** with only **25%** increase in labor; **eliminated** production set-up time.

	Sales	Pretax Net Profit	Models	Model Families	Average Lot Size	Productivity
2010	$10.1M	10.1%	10	6	6.4	95.1%
2008	$6.2M	(9.3%)	3	2	4.4	79%

- Earned sole-supplier status with John Deere; built construction-equipment business from **$0** to **$3M.**

- Eliminated an unprofitable OEM product line after aggressive attempts to revitalize the line were unsuccessful. Maintained favorable relationship with the customer.

Engineering Manager, 2007–2008

System design, development, testing, manufacture, commercial input | 3 staff

Served as primary customer contact in landing $1.3M in sales and a new customer for the Division.

Manufacturing Engineer, 2004–2007

Education

Six Sigma Black Belt, 2014: BigBox, Inc.
MBA, 2013: Loyola of Baltimore
BS Operations Management, 2004: University of Maryland

To: Jobs@GraysonManufacturing.com
From: c.chandler@gmail.com
Subject: Manufacturing Production Manager

As Plant Manager for a division of Xylon Medical, I led my facility to #1 in operational excellence among 14 global sites, based on results like these:

- ✓ Reduced production cycle from 50 days to 3.
- ✓ Boosted inventory turns from 4 to 11.
- ✓ Saved $400K yearly by training and certifying line workers to inspect their own goods.
- ✓ Doubled output in 3 months while adhering to some of the industry's most stringent production standards (ISO 9001 and FDA GMP).

Most recently, I led Lean/Six Sigma projects that delivered immediate savings of $300K and are projecting more than $1M in savings over 10 years.

I am very interested in your Manufacturing Production Manager position. May we meet soon to discuss how I can help your plants become leaner, more efficient, and more profitable?

Sincerely,

Chris Chandler
****
387-555-1234
c.chandler@gmail.com
http://www.linkedin.com/in/chrischandler

Keyword Answers to Interview Questions

Tell me about yourself.

Building top-performing manufacturing operations is my expertise. When I was challenged to orchestrate a Greenfield production plant for Simmons, I was able to staff the facility, install the equipment, design the manufacturing flow, and get the first product out the door within three months.

Originally joining Simmons to manage a complex turnaround at its largest plant, I introduced leading-edge manufacturing processes, including work cells, continuous flow, and cycle-time reductions, and we exceeded all of our objectives for the turnaround in the first year.

Currently as plant manager of a high-growth manufacturer, I am spearheading the introduction of advanced robotics, ISO 14000, a sophisticated master scheduling program, and a number of other high-profile initiatives. In summary, I am the executive who gets things done, increases revenues, improves profits, and drives long-term growth.

What is the most valuable skill you bring to our company?

The greatest value I bring to your organization is the diversity of my experience … from start-ups to turnarounds to high-growth production plants.

Each of these types of organizations has its own unique challenges and opportunities. It has been my responsibility to identify the challenges, implement effective solutions, and capitalize on opportunities that allowed us to grow, improve our bottom-line profit performance, and dominate the markets in which we have operated.

What is your most significant achievement?

When I arrived at Simmons Plastics Production, the company was in crisis. Costs were out of control, technologies weren't working, the management team had resigned itself to mediocrity, and customers were running out the door.

At that point, I recruited new management talent, brought in experts to resolve the technological issues, and launched a massive public relations effort to recapture our lost market share. Within one year, I was able to halt losses, increase revenues 42%, cut costs 25%, and regain better than 90% of our original customer base.

Chapter 18

Marketing

Top 100 Keywords

Analytics

B2B Marketing

B2C Marketing

Brand Building

Brand Management

Brand Strategy

Business Development

Buying Trends

Campaigns

Category Management

Category Marketing

Communications

Competitive Analysis

Competitive Market Intelligence

Consumer Behavior

Contract Negotiations

Corporate Communications

Corporate Identity

Corporate Image

Creative Design

Creative Media

Creative Writing

Data Collection & Analysis

Dealer Network Management

Demand Forecasting

Demographic Analysis

Digital Communications

Digital Marketing

Economic Analysis

Electronic Commerce

Emerging Markets

Global Markets

Government Relations

Graphic Design

Inbound Marketing

Incentive Campaigns

International Marketing

International Trade

Internet Marketing

Lead Generation

Market Assessment

Market Characteristics

Market Conditions

Market Development

Market Intelligence

Market Launch

Market Positioning

Market Research & Analysis

Market Share

Market Strategy

Market Trends

Marketing

Marketing Budget

Marketing Campaign

Marketing Communications

Marketing Management

Marketing Message

Marketing Plan

Marketing Strategy

Mass Marketing

Media Relations

Multimedia Advertising

Multimedia Marketing Campaign

Multimedia Marketing
  Communications

New Market Development

New Product Development

New Service Delivery

Negotiations

Niche Market

Online Marketing

Outbound Marketing

Press Relations

Product Development

Product Launch

Product Licensing

Product Line Extension

Product Marketing

Product Packaging

Product Pricing

Profitability Analysis

Project Management

Promotions

Public Relations

Publicity

Risk Assessment & Mitigation

Social Media

Software Solutions

Special Events

Statistical Analysis & Reporting

Strategic Communications Plan

Strategic Market Planning

Survey Design & Administration

Tactical Marketing

Team Building & Leadership

Technology

Telecommunications

Telemarketing

Trade Shows

Trend Analysis

Website Marketing

Cynthia Williams

336-949-1101 — cynwilliams@gmail.com
http://www.linkedin.com/in/cynthiawilliams

Marketing & Business Development Manager

Technology Evaluation & Commercialization

Marketing Leader with 12 years of success creating strategic marketing programs and business plans to support new products, new technologies, and business expansions.

MBA focused on technology commercialization and new product development.

Education

MBA, May 2016   NORTH CAROLINA STATE UNIVERSITY, Raleigh, NC
Concentration in Technology Evaluation & Commercialization; New Product Development

Key Projects and Activities

- **Medical Equipment Redesign:** Client firm requested help in redesigning sterilization component to outperform competitors. With team, defined 2 design options and developed overall marketing plan that lowered production costs and identified 3 potential new markets.

- **Disruptive Technology Evaluation & Product Commercialization:** With team, evaluated technology for commercial applications; identified opportunities in medical and high-tech industries; created business plan to bring products to market (currently in development phase).

- **Project Activities:** Technology Assessment; Market Research; Legal Analysis; Operational Analysis; Team & Organizational Analysis; Financial Analysis; New Business Financing Options.

- **Relevant Courses:** Product Design & Development; Technology Evaluation & Commercialization; Technology, Law & the Internet; High Tech Entrepreneurship; Innovation & Management.

BS Business Administration, 2003   UNIVERSITY OF RHODE ISLAND, Kingston, RI
Specialization in Marketing and Human Resources Management

Professional Experience

RALEIGH REGIONAL MEDICAL CENTER, Raleigh, NC   2013–Present
Marketing Manager: Oncology Services, Neurosciences Services, Primary Care, Urgent Care
Build visibility, brand awareness, and consumer preference for 4 service lines. Identify market opportunities and develop/execute marketing and public relations strategies, leading cross-functional teams and directing outside agencies. Track effectiveness of campaigns through evaluative studies and data analysis. Manage $1M budget.

- **Digital Strategy:** Shifted 20% of resources from traditional to online, video, audio, mobile apps, and social media. Increased digital capabilities and added processes to measure ROI.

- **CRM:** Improved data integrity, data integration, results tracking, and ROI analysis of marketing campaigns. For the first time, created an accurate database of doctors integrated across entire system.

- **Website Management:** Increased site visits more than 10% by strengthening SEO, adding banner ad capabilities, revamping the physician finder, and bringing multiple sites under the RMC umbrella.

- **Program Innovation:** Launched cardiovascular screening program to identify potential heart patients and channel them into the system. Screened 500 and introduced 120 into system in first 6 months.

- **Strategic Pilot Program Leadership:** Played a key role in developing and launching innovative MD360 pilot to establish distinctive physical footprint and culture for Urgent and Primary Care practices. Spearheaded marketing strategy and execution including media buys, website development, and product refinement. In 2015 assumed full marketing leadership for both practices.

CYNTHIA WILLIAMS

336-949-1101 — cynwilliams@gmail.com

HEALTH QC, INC., Cary, NC   2011–2013

Senior Associate for Marketing and Strategic Planning

Directed marketing, market research, advertising, public relations, new product development, and strategic planning initiatives for healthcare quality-improvement organization.

- **Growth Strategy:** Created new business plan that drove 10% growth/month in Professional Consulting Division. More than doubled account base. Reduced reliance on 2 primary accounts from 70% to 40% of the business while increasing sales in each of those key accounts.

- **Industry Outreach:** Launched public relations initiative to develop relationships with medical societies and hospital associations.

- **Marketing Communications:** Refined private-venture marketing communications and advertising to incorporate an external versus internal focus and increase reader appeal.

- **Business Innovation:** Conceived new business service that brought Health QC into an entirely new market segment and generated more than $500K revenue in 2 years.

STRATEGY PARTNERS, LLC, Seattle, WA   2004–2011

Senior Consultant

Designed, managed, and delivered marketing consulting services to clients in diverse industries. Conducted case planning and management, data analysis, report writing, client presentations, survey design and testing, marketing interviews, and data quality assurance. Representative assignments:

- **CRM:** Customer satisfaction measurement through data gathering, analysis, and approach modeling.

- **Process Redesign:** Distribution logistics analysis and development of a reengineered process for Fortune 50 client.

- **Sales Force Optimization:** Analysis and recommendations to improve effectiveness and efficiency of client's national sales force.

- **Market Entry Strategy:** Detailed plans to launch technology products and services and new markets.

SEA-TAC MANAGEMENT CONSULTANTS, INC., Tacoma, WA   2003–2004

Research Associate

Conducted market research studies and presented results to clients. Served as project manager, supervising information gathering and data analysis. Managed sales and promotional program: developed leads, made sales calls, and prepared and tracked proposals.

Professional Affiliations

Piedmont Entrepreneurs Network
Carolinas Society for Healthcare Planning and Marketing
Society for Healthcare Strategy and Market Development

Michael Van Der Beek

Toledo, OH 49382   444-323-9283
michaelvanderbeek@yahoo.com

February 14, 2016

Larry Nelson, VP Marketing
Martinson Products, Inc.
909 Toledo Avenue
Toledo, OH 49322

Dear Mr. Nelson:

Marketing is one of the most vital components to any consumer products venture. With both global competition and new product roll-outs at an all-time high, it is no longer enough to simply develop a great product. What is required is an astute marketer with deep consumer insight. And that is precisely who I am.

Working with some of the world's leading consumer companies, I have led innovative marketing programs with responsibility for product launches, new market expansions, and rebranding efforts. Most significant have been my financial results:

- For Jergens, I led the launch of 8 new products that generated annual revenues in excess of $20M.
- For ATMAN, I increased European market sales from $2M to $10M.
- For Stanley Products, I drove a rebranding of the home-products line that won "Best Marketing Campaign" at the 2013 Consumer Products Show.

These achievements are indicative of the quality and caliber of my entire professional career. I identify market opportunities, create winning marketing strategies, and develop profitable sales and marketing programs.

Since leaving Jergens last year, I have continued to focus my efforts on consumer products marketing and would be pleased to share specific engagements with you during an interview. Currently, I am exploring new career opportunities and would be delighted to meet with you.

Sincerely,

Michael Van Der Beek

Enclosure

Keyword Answers to Interview Questions

Tell me about yourself.

I'm the person who builds marketing organizations that far surpass everyone's expectations. In intensely competitive consumer product markets, I have defined market strategy and positioning, created portfolios of multimedia marketing and advertising communications, built high-profile press contacts, and utilized social media tools to their fullest.

I started my career with Johnson & Johnson—a great training ground for anyone in marketing. I then moved to Kellogg's, where I was able to turn around and re-build marketing organizations in three of their highest volume business units.

Currently, I'm the marketing director for Emerson Products, where I created a new, multimedia marketing organization that helped drive our growth from start-up to more than $20 million in annual sales in just three years.

What is the most valuable skill you bring to our company?

Understanding the marketplace and the competition is what makes me so successful in my job. Before we can create a marketing strategy, we must first build our knowledge about the target market, customer demographics, competitors, and economic influences. It's only then that we can design what will work for that company or product in that market segment.

Equally important are my skills in creative concept and design. Although I have a team that manages most of those efforts, I still enjoy the actual process of developing new marketing communications. Perhaps my greatest talent is writing press releases that have consistently garnered major media attention.

What is your most significant achievement?

I've already mentioned my contributions to the financial success of my current employer—growth from start-up to $20 million in less than three years. That achievement is indicative of my successes throughout my career, most significantly with Kellogg's, where my greatest achievements were for the Keebler business unit.

When Keebler faced declining sales volumes, I helped to re-strategize and redesign consumer marketing outreach efforts—print, broadcast, online, and social media. We reversed the downward spiral and put the business on a path toward 15% annual growth for the next five years. With a product volume as large as Keebler's, that's a huge financial gain for the corporation.

Chapter 19

Public Relations and Corporate Communications

Top 100 Keywords

Advertising Communications

Advocacy

Agency Relations

Board of Directors
Communications

Brand Image & Identity

Brand Management

Brand Strategy

Broadcast Journalism

Broadcast Media

Budget Development &
Management

Business Development

Campaign Management

Client Communications

Client Relationship Management

Communications Management

Communications Media

Communications Strategy

Community Affairs

Community Outreach

Computer Graphics

Conference Planning &
Management

Corporate Communications

Corporate Identity

Corporate Outreach

Corporate Sponsorship

Creative Media

Creative Services

Creative Writing

Crisis Communications

Crisis Management

Cross-Cultural Communications

Customer Communications

Demographic Data Analysis

Design

Digital Media

Direct Mail Campaign

E-Commerce

Economic Trends & Forecasting

Editing

Electronic Advertising

Electronic Media

Employee Communications

Employee Relations

Event Planning & Management

Exhibits

Focus Groups

Government Affairs

Graphic Design

Grassroots Campaign

Internal Communications

Investor Communications

Issues Management

Journalism

Legislative Affairs

Management Communications

Market Research

Marketing Communications

Marketing Message

Media Buys

Media Interviews

Media Placement

Media Relations

Media Scheduling

Meeting Planning

Merchandising

Multimedia Communications

New Business Development

New Market Development

New Product Introduction

News Release

Online Content Development

Political Action Committee (PAC)

Political Affairs

PowerPoint Presentations

Premiums

Presentations

Press Conference

Press Release

Print Communications

Print Journalism

Print Media

Product Launch

Project Management

Promotions

Public Affairs

Public Outreach

Public Policy

Public Relations

Publications

Publicity

Sales Incentives

Shareholder Communications

Social Media

Special Events

Strategic Communications Plan

Strategic Positioning

Technology

Trade Shows

VIP Relations

Writing

REBECCA CORCORAN

rebecca@corcoran.com ... 206–215-862-9724 ... LinkedIn.com/in/rebeccacorcoran

Marketing / Media & Public Relations / Special Events / Sporting Events

**Creating High-Impact Images, Concepts, Services, Programs & Opportunities
To Build Revenues, Corporate Sponsorships & Fundraising Contributions**

PR professional with in-depth experience leading the conceptualization, creative design, planning, staffing, budgeting, and promotion of marketing and special event programs worldwide. Expert in identifying market demand and building sustainable market presence.

Professional Experience

Senior Associate   THE POLETTI GROUP, Seattle, WA   2012–Present

Invited to join an elite event-management organization specializing in high-profile fundraising and special events. Manage all facets of major programs, including these highlights:

- **Shreiber Hospital Charity Luncheon**, 2015—one of the largest and most widely covered events in the region. Increased fundraising by 25%. Selected to chair the 2016 event.

- **Science Service Campaign,** 2014—well-publicized event launched to increase awareness of the innovative science scholarship and academic opportunities sponsored by the organization. Created a series of dynamic marketing and public relations materials to increase market visibility. Worked collaboratively with Honorary Chairperson Melinda Gates.

- **Annual Red Cross Ball**, 2012–2015—Prominent social event with celebrity sponsors. Increased attendance from 250 in 2012 to 800+ in 2015. Added 6 major corporate sponsors and secured multi-year commitments from all 6.

PR & Events Director   LAKE WASHINGTON POLO & COUNTRY CLUB, Seattle, WA   2010–2012

Directed integrated PR, marketing, special events, media, and promotions programs for the Club, the Polo Museum, and internationally sponsored sporting events. Held concurrent responsibility for spearheading national and international real estate sales, marketing, and PR programs for Equestrian Estates (high-end residential sub-community). Ranked as the #1 revenue producer.

- Appointed to **Advisory Board** for Polo Museum. Led successful fundraising and and high-profile PR campaigns.

- Organized and executed an 800-person **Grand Opening** celebration that captured national and international media coverage.

General Manager / Co-Founder   GRAY TRAVEL AGENCY, Seattle, WA   2005–2010

Co-founded a unique travel and tour company with market focus on major specialty and sporting events worldwide (Melbourne Cup, Olympics, World Championships). Designed distinctive tour packages for corporate clients, groups, and associations. Personally managed daily agency operations, staffing, sales/marketing, customer service, contract negotiations, and multimedia PR campaigns.

- Built business to **$4M** in annual sales.

Professional Activities & Affiliations

- **Independent Consultant** retained by Gross & Co. (2015 to Present), a newly formed investment banking firm, to provide expertise in **investor solicitation and negotiations** for a new $42M fund. Travelled with partners to Europe to meet with potential investors. Currently creating a portfolio of PR, marketing, and business development materials.

- **Special Events & Tour Consultant** with Elite Travel Services, Palm Beach, FL (2010–Present). Develop and market unique travel packages to upscale resorts, sporting events, and fundraising events worldwide. Current program includes Princess Grace Foundation, Monte Carlo; FIFA World Cup; and 2016 Olympic Games in Brazil.

- **Founding Board Member** of Equestrian Events, Inc., a non-profit organization formed by the Governor of Kentucky. Launched high-profile PR campaigns, special events, fundraising programs, and corporate sponsorships. Served as President for 2 terms, Vice President for 2 terms, and Secretary for 2 terms. Built fundraising budget from $15K to $450K over 8 years.

Education

Bachelor of Arts, Speech & Hearing Pathology / Graduate Studies—UNIVERSITY OF KENTUCKY, Lexington, KY

JOSEPH COLLINS

joecollins75@gmail.com
412-345-6710

June 10, 2016

Margaret McAdams
Vice President Corporate Communications
PNC Bank
9450 Victory Parkway
Pittsburgh, PA 15203

Dear Ms. McAdams:

Andrea Shay suggested that I get in touch with you as I recently relocated from Washington DC to my hometown of Pittsburgh and am looking to build my network. Because we are both in the field of corporate communications, Andrea thought we should be connected.

For the past 20 years, my affiliations with top-tier organizations such as **Verizon,** the **White House,** and **CVent** have provided opportunities to deliver effective programs and services in challenging environments:

➤ With Verizon for 10 years, multiple acquisitions and high-profile service issues presented the need for sensitive yet forthright communications with our employees and the media.

➤ At the White House, crisis management and message crafting were the order of the day—requiring poise and professionalism under high pressure and tight deadlines.

➤ As event manager for CVent's largest annual program—an international user conference with 7000 attendees—I gained the full confidence of the executive management team by delivering complex, multi-day programs without a visible hitch.

I am currently seeking a new corporate communications role in Pittsburgh and would appreciate hearing your thoughts and recommendations. I will call within a few days to see what suggestions you might be able to offer. Perhaps I can take you to lunch as a thank-you for your help.

Best regards,

Joseph Collins

enclosure

Keyword Answers to Interview Questions

Tell me about yourself.

For the past 12 years, I've been responsible for the strategic design and tactical execution of a full range of public relations programs—programs targeted to our corporate and institutional clients, programs targeted to the general public for our retail division, and programs to increase media awareness and coverage. My expertise lies in my ability to coordinate project teams encompassing creative and graphic design, strategy, and field implementation.

As a result of my efforts and those of other PR professionals in the organization, we have increased our market awareness, strengthened customer loyalty, expanded the reach of our corporate identity campaigns, and built a robust social media presence.

I love the challenge of PR—the puzzle of how to build positive awareness through influence and education, how to share what's great about our company, our products, and our people. Of course, dealing with the inevitable negative stories is also critical, and I find that having a strong base of positive support makes those occasional "downs" much easier to manage.

What is the most valuable skill you bring to our company?

Undeniably, my greatest strength is my ability to assemble and lead project teams through all facets of campaign design and execution. Whether working with a small group of 3–4 individuals or a multi-divisional team of 20+, I have consistently provided the leadership necessary to achieve project milestones. I manage by consensus, rewarding each individual team member for his or her contributions to the overall project.

Just as important, however, let me also mention that I have outstanding oral and written communication skills, a must for every PR professional.

What is your most significant achievement?

I am most proud of my work on the Smart-Home launch campaign. Working with a team of 12 other PR and corporate communication experts, we designed a multimedia campaign, integrating print, television, radio, and online channels to facilitate a global market launch.

As a result of our efforts, in tandem with those of the field sales organization, we far exceeded our initial revenue goals, bringing in more than $12 million in Smart-Home sales within the first 60 days.

Chapter 20

Purchasing, Warehousing, and Logistics

Top 100 Keywords

Acquisition Management

Asset Management

Barter Trade

Bid Review

Buy vs. Lease Analysis

Capital Equipment Acquisition

Cargo Carrier

Cargo Handling

Carrier Management

Claims

Commodities

Common Carrier

Competitive Bidding

Container Transportation

Contract Administration

Contract Change Order

Contract Negotiations

Contract Terms & Conditions

Contract Transportation

Cost Control & Savings

Cradle-to-Grave Procurement

Customer Delivery

Dedicated Logistics

Demand Analysis & Planning

Dispatch Operations

Distribution

Driver Leasing

Durable Goods

Efficiency Improvement

Equipment Control

Export

Facilities Management

Fixed-Price Contracts

Fleet Management

Freight Consolidation

Freight Forwarding

Hazardous Materials (HAZMAT)

Import

Inbound

Integrated Logistics Management

Integrated Supply Chain

Intermodal Transportation

International Sourcing

International Trade

Inventory Planning & Control

Just-in-Time (JIT) Purchasing

Leasing

Less-Than-Truckload (LTL)

Logistics

Materials Management

Materials Movement

Materials Replenishment
    Ordering (MRO) Purchasing

Multi-Site Operations

Negotiation

Non-Durable Goods

Offshore Purchasing

Order Expediting

Order Processing

Outbound

Outsource

Perishable Goods

Price Analysis & Negotiations

Procurement

Product Availability

Product Returns

Productivity Improvement

Proposal Review

Purchase Orders

Purchasing

Purchasing Contracts

Purchasing Specifications

Regulatory Compliance

Request for Proposal (RFP)

Request for Quotation (RFQ)

Requisition

Retail Trade

Route Planning & Management

Safety

Sourcing

Space Optimization

Specifications

Strategic Sourcing

Subcontractor Negotiations

Supplier Availability

Supplier Management

Supplier Quality

Supplier Sourcing

Supply Chain Management

Technology

Terminal Operations

Trade

Transportation

Trucking

Vendor Negotiations

Vendor Quality

Warehouse Operations

Warehousing

Wholesale Trade

Workflow Optimization

Yield

Suzanna Reynolds

Tampa, FL 33598   linkedin.com/in/suzyreynolds
897-314-5431—Call or Text   suzy.reynolds@yahoo.com

Purchasing Leader

More than 15 years' experience managing **PURCHASING / MATERIALS MANAGEMENT / INVENTORY CONTROL**
operations. Qualifications include:

- Purchasing Department Management
- Staffing / Training / Supervision
- Quality / Productivity Improvement
- Inventory Planning / Forecasting

- Vendor Sourcing / Vendor Selection
- Contract Negotiations / Contract Administration
- Competitive Bidding / Bid Management
- Cost Reduction / Cost Avoidance

Certified Purchasing Manager (CPM) Candidate

Professional Experience

PREMIERE MANUFACTURING, INC., Tampa, FL ~ 2010–2016

Purchasing Manager—Southeast (2012–2016)
Global Vendor Sourcing ~ Vendor Contract Negotiations ~ Materials Planning ~ Inventory Analysis
8 Direct Reports, 27 Indirect Personnel ~ $100M+ Annual Spend

- Managed purchasing operations during a period of significant growth, as purchase orders increased from 12,000 to 40,000 annually and line items surged from 4,000 to 110,000. Delivered significant recurring financial gains:

  - $400K reduction in annual payroll expense by realigning workforce and reducing staff from 35 to 22.
  - $75K savings in office supply and material costs through aggressive vendor negotiations.
  - $1M new revenue through innovative program to refurbish and resell equipment and sell scrap.

- Launched new Materials Forecasting Department to more effectively manage materials planning functions for company operations across the Southeast.

- Led design and implementation of a paperless purchasing and invoicing system that significantly upgraded the productivity, efficiency, and quality of the entire materials management organization.

- Negotiated development and subsequently managed administration of a cooperative educational program with Tampa Technical Institute for start-up of a CPM Certification Program for Premiere personnel.

Purchasing Agent (2010–2012)
Vendor Research ~ Sourcing~ Bidding ~ Documentation ~ $1.7M Annually in JIT Purchasing

- Scheduled and purchased all materials for press switches, solenoids, mini-pressure transducers, and molding department—stampings, metals, copper, brass, stainless steel, screw machine components, molded parts, tooling.

- Reduced R&D purchasing costs $200K for one specific project (20% under projected costs).

- Saved $150K in costs on plastic components through negotiation of bulk purchasing agreements.

- Lowered product inventories more than 25% annually ($250K estimated savings).

Suzanna Reynolds   897-314-5431 ~ suzy.reynolds@yahoo.com

MELLON SYSTEMS, INC., Tampa, FL ~ 2009–2010

Senior Buyer
Purchasing ~ Vendor Sourcing ~ Materials Management

- Managed purchasing for a diversity of commodities—primary electro/electromechanical products and metal-fabricated materials, cabinetry, plant equipment, maintenance and repair supplies—for both the manufacturing and land/building divisions of the company.
- Held concurrent responsibility for research, selection, and contracting with technical service consultants.

STEWART OFFICE SUPPLY, Ft. Myers, FL ~ 2007–2009

Sales Representative
Sales of Office Equipment, Furniture & Supplies ~ Commercial, Industrial & Institutional Accounts

- Met with prospective clients to evaluate product requirements, delivered sales presentations, negotiated pricing, and closed final sales.
- Consistently met monthly quotas for sales revenues and new account development.

Education

TAMPA TECHNICAL INSTITUTE
30 credit hours toward CPM Certification

NATIONAL MANAGEMENT ASSOCIATION
Management Training & Supervisory Development Courses

PREMIER MANUFACTURING, INC.
Management, Supervisory, Communications & Performance Development Courses

Dana Whitehouse
469-678-1019
danawhitehouse@mac.com

March 26, 2016

Charles Abbington
Vice President of Operations
Bechtold Corporation
294 Washington Avenue
Dallas, TX 87451

Dear Mr. Abbington:

I understand from your Round Rock plant manager, Dave Cannavaro, that you are looking to add a few top-notch professionals to your purchasing organization.

With 12 years' experience in purchasing management and material/supply sourcing, I offer strong qualifications and a record of consistent achievement in:

➢ Negotiating multimillion-dollar, multi-year purchasing contracts—long term, fixed price, and minority supplier.
➢ Identifying quality suppliers and establishing favorable pricing, terms, and conditions.
➢ Transferring supply contracts from foreign to domestic sources to meet stringent quality and performance requirements.
➢ Directing sophisticated manufacturing engineering and tooling programs.

Most notably, I have captured millions of dollars in cost savings, including:

➢ $20 million purchasing cost reduction for Venture Systems.
➢ $5.5 million purchasing cost reduction for Chrysler Corporation.

I am most proud of my tenure with Venture Systems. Recruited from Chrysler in 2011, I built the purchasing function from concept into a 10-person global business unit managing $550 million in annual spend. Our financial and operational successes were notable and included the introduction of innovative business strategies, best-in-class procurement policies, and strategic vendor alliances.

Currently, I am exploring new professional opportunities and was quite impressed with what Dave told me about your company culture and growth plans. I would welcome the opportunity to meet with you at your earliest convenience. Thank you.

Sincerely,

Dana Whitehouse

Enclosure: Resume

Keyword Answers to Interview Questions

Tell me about yourself.

I am a well-qualified purchasing manager with 15 years' experience in the automotive industry with Ford and Chevrolet. During my tenure with these companies, my scope of responsibility has increased dramatically. Initially only responsible for purchasing electronic and mechanical components, I soon added vendor sourcing in both domestic and international markets. Following that assignment, I was trained in and assumed responsibility for all vendor contract terms and conditions.

Now, as one of only six purchasing managers in a $500 million production facility, I manage the entire supply chain, including inventory planning and control, vendor quality assurance, contracts, purchasing, and the flow of materials throughout the complex. In fact, last year I purchased more than $68 million in raw materials, technologies, and components!

What is the most valuable skill you bring to our company?

My negotiating skills are by far my strongest attribute. I NEVER accept the first price I'm given, knowing that if I can strategically negotiate, I will always be able to reduce material costs.

Hand-in-hand with negotiating is my ability to communicate. Being able to build rapport and develop cooperative working relationships has been at the foundation of my success in negotiating and in fostering the long-term, profitable management of our purchasing and supply chain management operations.

What is your most significant achievement?

Without a doubt, my most significant contributions to both Ford and Chevrolet have been my successes in cost reduction. Most notably, Ford was paying more than $2.5 million annually for a small electronic component. By sourcing another vendor and negotiating a multi-year contract, I was able to reduce that cost by 25% each year.

With Chevrolet, I've delivered more than $12 million in annual cost savings on several core components and am projecting an additional $5 million savings on all technology expenditures over the next two years.

Chapter 21

Real Estate and Property Management

Top 100 Keywords

Americans with Disabilities Act (ADA)

Apartment

Appraisal

Appreciation

Architecture

Architectural Drawing

Architectural Rendering

Assessment

Asset Disposition

Asset Management

Asset Valuation

Asset Workout & Recovery

Association Dues

Brokerage

Buyer

Buyer-Seller Negotiations

Capital Improvement

Closing Statement

Closings

Code Compliance

Commercial Development

Commercial Property

Community Association

Condominium

Condominium Association

Contract Negotiations

Cooperative

Deed

Demographic Analysis

Density

Depreciation

Divestiture

Economic Development

Energy Efficiency
    Escrow

Facilities Management

Fair Housing Laws

Fair Market Value

Flood Map

Flood Plain

Funds Disbursement

Grounds Maintenance

Historic Preservation

Historic Renovation

Home Inspection

Home Warranty

Homeowner

Homeowners Association

Income Potential

Inspections

Land Acquisition

Land Development

Land Financing

Landowner

Leasing

Legal Descriptiions

Lender Relations

Listings

Loan Processing

Maintenance Engineering

Master Community Association

Mixed-Use Property

Model Home

Mortgage Banking

Mortgage Lending

Multi-Unit Property

Occupancy Rate

On-Site Management

Pre-Qualification

Preventive Maintenance

Property Closing

Property Financing

Property Legal Description

Property Maintenance & Repair

Property Management

Property Valuation

Public Records

Real Estate Appraisal

Real Estate Brokerage

Real Estate Closing

Real Estate Development

Real Estate Investment Trust (REIT)

Real Estate Law

Real Estate Partnership

Real Property

Regulatory Compliance & Reporting

Renovation

Rental Property

Rental Terms & Conditions

Residential Development

Residential Property

Return on Investment (ROI)

Sales Contract

Seller

Syndication

Tenant Relations

Tenant Retention

Urban Planning

Valuation

Zoning Bylaws

Zoning Regulations

Karen Richards, RPA

karichards@gmail.com • 601-538-3229 • LinkedIn.com/in/karichards

REAL ESTATE INDUSTRY PROFESSIONAL
Property Management / Marketing / Tenant Relations

15 Years' Experience in Commercial & Residential Real Estate

Increasing Revenues, Occupancy & Income • Directing Property Construction & Renovations
Negotiating Leases • Reducing Costs • Increasing Tenant Satisfaction & Retention

PROFESSIONAL EXPERIENCE

Property Manager   **A-ONE PROPERTIES, INC.**, Clifton, MO   2013–Present

Portfolio: 163,000 SF of prime office space in a 3-building complex on 9 acres. Asset value of $13.5M.

Recruited as Property Manager with full P&L responsibility for the entire portfolio. Scope of responsibility includes construction, renovation, tenant relations/retention, collections, outsourcing, contract negotiations, purchasing, budgeting, monthly financial reporting, and general office/administrative affairs. Manage 15 staff.

* Increased occupancy from **29%** to **73%** in less than 3 years.
* Managed **$1.5M** renovation of all common areas. Delivered project on time and within budget.
* Negotiated outsourcing contracts for facilities maintenance/repair, janitorial services, and property security. Lowered operating costs **7%** while increasing quality of service and tenant satisfaction.

Property Manager   **THE REAL PROPERTY CORPORATION,** Lewis, MO   2011–2013

Portfolio: 230,000 SF comprising 3 office buildings and 11 luxury garden apartment complexes. Asset value of $36M.

Led successful turnaround of the portfolio to meet investor and owner financial objectives. Directed marketing, construction and renovation, tenant relations, cash flow management, financial reporting, and general administrative affairs. Worked with architects and contractors in the space planning and tenant fit-up of all leased space.

* Spearheaded a high-profile marketing and public relations initiative to upgrade tenant quality.
* Completed large-scale upgrade of facilities, properties, and common areas on time and **2%** under budget.
* Reduced expenditures **18%** through a new preventive maintenance program and close oversight of all maintenance and improvement work—electrical systems, HVAC, elevators, and grounds.

Project Manager   **GRIFFITH MANAGEMENT CORPORATION,** Wayne, MO   2010–2011

Portfolio: Mid-sized commercial office building. Asset value of $4.5M.

Recruited for year-long special project to oversee a complete facilities renovation. Directed a number of site improvement projects, expanded and upgraded existing spaces, and designed tenant/owner communication programs.

* Increased occupancy **35%** through extension of existing leases and capture of new, long-term tenants.
* Increased property value **28%** in 1 year.

Broker/Property Manager   **ROBINSON GROUP, INC.,** Montclair, MO   2001–2010

Represented sellers, buyers, and investors in commercial real estate sales transactions totaling several million dollars. Served as property manager for Robinson Group's investment properties.

EDUCATION & PROFESSIONAL CERTIFICATIONS

Certified Property Manager (CPM) Candidate, Institute of Real Estate Management, Current
Real Property Administrator (RPA), Building Owners and Managers Association, 2001
Registered Property Manager (RPM), International Real Estate Institute, 2000
Missouri Licensed Real Estate Broker, Since 2001

PROFESSIONAL AFFILIATIONS

National Association of Corporate Real Estate Executives (NACORE)   Institute of Real Estate Management (IREM)
Building Owners and Managers Association International (BOMA)   International Real Estate Institute (IREI)

MORGAN J. CARTER

Baltimore, MD 21212
410.444.8736 ~ morgan.carter@gmail.com
http://www.LinkedIn.com/in/morganjcarter

May 1, 2016

John Warner, President
Fidelity Capital Ventures
1000 Michigan Avenue
Washington, DC 22002

Dear Mr. Warner:

Knowing of your extensive activity in real estate development—specifically large-scale, mixed-used construction projects—I believe you will be interested in my qualifications.

- 20+ years' experience in real estate development and management in the US and international markets.
- Complete development and management responsibility for $500M in projects over the past 10 years.
- Leadership of more than $450M in project funding and public/private partnership financing programs.

Most significant, however, is my ability to drive projects through complex community, political, and governmental channels. By providing a strong community vision and decisive action plan, I have won the support of community, political, business, and financial leaders—support that is critical to project funding, development, and profitable sale/leasing.

I would welcome the chance to explore potential opportunities with your firm, and I appreciate your time in reviewing my qualifications. Thank you.

Sincerely,

Morgan J. Carter

Enclosure

Keyword Answers to Interview Questions

Tell me about yourself.

Currently, I'm the #1 real estate sales associate for residential sales and the #4 associate for commercial sales in the Dallas metro Keller Real Estate organization. I achieved this distinction through years of hard work and dedication to the industry. It's now my goal to move to a larger organization where I can deliver even stronger results and manage higher-dollar transactions.

Having the privilege of working with homeowners, helping them to find the house of their dreams, is remarkably rewarding. However, I'm just as enthusiastic—and successful—handling complicated, multi-party negotiations for commercial development projects. It's wonderful to watch a project move from concept to funding through construction and grand opening.

Prior to my career in real estate, I was a successful sales associate with a mid-size consumer products company, where my responsibilities entailed new client development, product demonstration, contract negotiations, and sales closing. I consistently achieved—and often surpassed—my sales goals.

What is the most valuable skill you bring to our company?

Without a doubt, my greatest talent is building relationships with prospective clients. When we first meet, it's my opportunity to serve them immediately. By focusing on their specific needs, desires, and expectations, we're able to accelerate the entire real estate sales process.

What's even more important, I'm able to create an environment of cooperation and trust with my clients, many of whom have had less than positive experiences with real estate agents in the past.

What is your most significant achievement?

Hand-in-hand with my strong skills in client relationship management are the resulting achievements. First, my clients are mine forever and always come back to me for whatever real estate needs they have in the future.

Second, my clients are a great referral source for me. In fact, I spend very little on advertising since my client load is always at a maximum as a direct result of referrals.

And, finally, I've been asked to speak before our local Chamber of Commerce on client development and retention, as my success is well known throughout the region—within real estate and many other industries.

Chapter 22

Retail

Top 100 Keywords

Advertising

Branch Stores

Brand

Brand Marketing

Brand Positioning

Brand Strategy

Budgeting

Buyer

Buyer Awareness

Buyer Behavior

Buyer Trends

Campaign Management

Cash Management

Cash Receipts

Cash Reconciliation

Catalog Sales

Category Management

Competitive Market Intelligence

Competitor Analysis

Computer Operations

Consumer Behavior

Consumer Packaged Goods

Credit

Customer Demographics

Customer Loyalty

Customer Satisfaction

Customer Segmentation

Customer Service

Data Collection & Analysis

Demographics

Direct Response Advertising

Displays

Distribution Channel

Distribution Management

Distributor Network

District Sales

E-Commerce

Hard Goods

In-Store Promotions

Incentive Campaign

Inventory Planning & Control

Inventory Shrinkage

Licensing

Loss Prevention

Market Research

Market Segmentation

Mass Merchandising

Mass Merchant

Merchandise Displays

Merchandise Movement

Merchandising

Multi-Site Operations

Multimedia Advertising

Order Fulfillment

Order Processing

Point-of-Sale (POS)

POS Promotions

Price Tags

Pricing

Product Demand

Product Demonstration

Product Line Extension

Product Management

Product Merchandising

Product Specifications

Profit & Loss (P&L) Management

Profitability Analysis

Project Management

Promotions

Public Relations

Rebate

Retail

Retail Advertising

Retail Operations

Retail Sales

Sales

Sales Forecasting

Sales Incentive

Sales Orders

Sales Receipts

Sales Reconciliations

Sales Reporting

Security

Social Media

Soft Goods

Software Solutions

Specialty Retail

Staffing

Stock Management

Store Management

Store Operations

Team Building & Leadership

Technology

Telemarketing

Training & Development

Trend Analysis

Vendor Relations

Warehousing

Website Sales

Wholesale

CHARLES BEAUCHESNE

514-675-8723   New Orleans, LA   CharlesLA@gmail.com

MULTI-SITE RETAIL MANAGER
Startup, Turnaround & High-Growth Organizations | Franchise and Company-Owned Operations
Operations Management | Business Planning | Human Resources | Marketing | Finance

Problem solver with strong "call-to-action" skills
who consistently delivers strong revenue and profit results in highly competitive markets.

PROFESSIONAL EXPERIENCE

REGIONAL MANAGER: Kwik Lube International, Inc., New Orleans, LA   2013–Present

Scope: P&L for 37 Corporate-Owned Sales/Service Centers | 4 District Manager Direct Reports | $50M Annual Sales

Challenge: Drive revenue growth, reduce operating costs, and improve net profitability of multi-site operations.

Actions & Results:
- Delivered **17%** sales increase and **13.3%** profit improvement in 2 years. Exceeded profit goal every year.
- Ranked the **#1** region in the U.S. for customer satisfaction.
- Strengthened accounting and financial management, bringing clarity and speed to monthly financial reporting.
- Launched management training and development program to elevate expertise within each center.
- Currently spearheading start-up of new strategic partnership with Sears (nationwide program). Leading the development of 3 pilot operations in Louisiana. Delivered **$300K** in first-year sales.

GENERAL MANAGER: Smith Petroleum (Kwik Lube Franchise), Metairie, LA   2008–2013

Scope: P&L for 11 Franchise Locations | 2 District Managers | $6M Annual Sales

Challenge: Build revenue and profitability by strengthening advertising and marketing, streamlining administrative processes, improving financial controls, and upgrading recruitment and training.

Actions & Results:
- Drove reorganization and operations redesign initiative across entire enterprise.
- In first year built sales from **$3.5M** to **$4.2M,** transitioned from loss to breakeven, and took negative cash flow to positive. Grew revenue to **$6M** in less than 5 years.
- Implemented networked POS technology to enhance internal sales controls and reporting capabilities.
- Designed incentive program and reduced operating costs by **$500K.**
- Hired local advertising agency and directed multimedia print, broadcast, and direct mail campaigns.

DIRECTOR OF OPERATIONS: Gulf Automotive (Kwik Lube Franchise), Baton Rouge, LA   2005–2008

Scope: P&L for 8 Franchise Locations | 2 District Managers | $3.5M Annual Sales

Challenge: Lead the franchisee through a period of rapid growth and expansion—build organizational infrastructure, strengthen operations, recruit/train personnel, and spearhead aggressive marketing and business development initiatives.

Actions & Results:
- Drove accelerated growth from **3** to **8** locations, **36** to **100+** employees, **$1.5M** to **$3.5M** in sales.
- Smoothly integrated **2** acquired Pennzoil operations into existing franchise.

KWIK LUBE INTERNATIONAL, INC.   2002–2005

Operations Consultant / Training Director (2004–2005) | **Operations Assistant** (2003–2004)
Unit Manager (2003) | **Manager Trainee** (2002–2003)

EDUCATION
BS Business Administration, Bridgewater College, Bridgewater, VA, 2002
The Dale Carnegie Course, 2004

To: Info@Jared.com
From: Davina Chu
Subject: Retail Sales Associate—allretailjobs.com

What I love most about retail sales: The opportunity to help customers find just the right item for an important occasion, a special gift, or a big celebration.

Knowing that customers come to Jared for exactly those reasons, I am very excited about pursuing a Retail Sales opportunity with your Wayside Galleria store.

My retail experience includes:

- **Consultative Sales:** For 5 years I helped customers choose finishes and upgrades for new home construction. I excel at listening, learning, and guiding customers through the sales process.

- **Feature and Benefit Presentations:** Every customer is different, and as a salesperson I focus on sharing details that will help everyone choose the product or service that's right for them.

- **Up-Sales of Extended Service Plans:** When recommending appliances, I made a convincing case (85% success rate) for purchasing extended warranties to ensure a trouble-free owner experience.

- **Teamwork:** I work well with other members of the sales team to create a great customer experience while meeting sales objectives. In all 5 years, we exceeded team goals by at least 10%.

The attached resume is a brief overview of my career and qualifications. I would love the opportunity for a personal interview to persuade you that I would be a great addition to your team.

Sincerely,

Davina Chu
****

davina.chu@gmail.com
857-554-1012

Keyword Answers to Interview Questions

Tell me about yourself.

At age 18, my very first job was as a sales associate with The Gap. Six months later, I was promoted to assistant store manager; nine months later to store manager, the youngest ever in the history of the company. Well, I was hooked!

I continued at The Gap part-time while attending the University of Michigan, where I earned my Bachelor's Degree in Retail Management. Following graduation, I was recruited to Saks Fifth Avenue, where I've now worked for five years and am currently the merchandising director for the Saks Fifth Avenue store in New York City. I love my job and my career, but I'm ready for more responsibility with a smaller, growth-driven, and innovative retailer such as Bonobos.

What is the most valuable skill you bring to our company?

My love of the industry is perhaps my greatest strength, along with my knowledge of virtually all retail operations … sales, buying, merchandising, customer service, promotions, special events, facilities management, security, inventory control, shrinkage, buyer awareness, and much more.

My career with both The Gap and Saks has given me an exceptionally strong experience across diverse retail operations. Let me also mention that I have very strong skills in employee training, development, and leadership.

What is your most significant achievement?

Personally speaking, my most significant achievement has been the rapid promotion of my career.

Professionally speaking, in my current position with Saks, I've reduced annual shrinkage by more than 12%, a huge decrease over previous years. While working with The Gap, I was able to increase annual sales by 15%–18% annually for four consecutive years.

Chapter 23

Sales

Top 100 Keywords

Account Development

Account Relationship
   Management

Account Retention

Brand

Brand Development

Brand Integrity

Brand Marketing

Budget Administration

Budget Management

Business Development

Buying Trends

Campaign Management

Category Management

Client Development

Client Loyalty

Client Management

Client Needs Assessment

Client Relationship Management

Client Retention

Client Satisfaction

Client Services

Cold Calling

Communications

Competitive Analysis

Competitive Market Intelligence

Consumer Behavior

Contracts

Copywriting

Corporate Branding

Corporate Image & Identity

Creative Design

Creative Media

Cross-Cultural Communications

Customer Care

Customer Communications

Customer Demographics

Customer Management

Customer Needs Assessment

Customer Relationship
   Management

Customer Retention

Customer Segmentation

Customer Service

Dealer

Demographic Analysis

Distribution Channels

Distributor Network Management

E-Business

E-Commerce

Economic Trends

Electronic Media

Global Markets

Headquarters Account
    Management

International Trade

Key Account Management

Licensing

Line Extension

Mass Merchants

Merchandising

Multi-Channel Distribution

Negotiations

New Business Development

New Market Development

New Product Development

Online Content Development

Order Processing & Fulfillment

Orders

Packaging

Point-of-Sales (POS)

Policies & Procedures

Presentations

Pricing

Print Communications

Private Branding

Private Label

Product Demand

Product Design & Development

Product Launch

Product Licensing

Product Line Extension

Product Management

Product Merchandising

Product Packaging

Product Pricing

Promotions

Public Relations

Retail Sales

Revenue Stream

Sales

Sales Orders

Segmentation

Social Media

Strategic Planning

Team Building & Leadership

Technology

Telecommunications

Trade Shows

Training & Development

Trend Analysis & Forecasting

Vendor Negotiations

Wholesale

STEPHEN X. GORDON

206-561-7612 • sgordon75@gmail.com
http://www.linkedin.com/in/stephenxgordon

SALES ▪ KEY ACCOUNT MANAGEMENT ▪ BUSINESS DEVELOPMENT

Top-performing sales professional with record of <u>always</u> exceeding sales, profit, and market-share goals.

▪ Consultative and solution-selling expert with proven ability to identify and capitalize on sales opportunities.

▪ Dedicated planner and goal setter, persistent prospector and cold-caller, talented presenter, and keen closer.

▪ Effective territory manager with strong customer relationship skills and ability to juggle multiple priorities.

PROFESSIONAL EXPERIENCE

XYZ CORPORATION *(NYSE: XYZ)*   Seattle, WA, 2013–Present
$5B public corporation, a leading distributor of building products to dealers, retailers, builders, and industrial users

▪ **Northwest Region Territory Manager—Industrial/Manufactured Housing**
Sales of Building Materials | Industrial & Manufactured Housing Accounts | Metro Seattle Territory

Create and execute sales/business plan for the territory, balancing new business development with account management and customer support. Work with a broad customer base (millwork houses, fixture/furniture/exhibit manufacturing facilities, cabinet manufacturers, concrete accessory and rebar customers), identifying needs and selling a diverse line of products/solutions.

- Achieved both sales and margin growth **every year** in a stagnant market.

	Sales	Gross Margin
2015	$8.4M	$971K
2014	$3.1M	$384K
2013	$1.9M	$185K

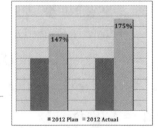

- Rose to **#9** nationwide, **#3** in region for gross margin increase in 2015.
- Prospected and developed more than **$1.2M** in new accounts.
- Developed just-in-time programs that controlled costs and streamlined inventory for key accounts while driving sales growth and margin increase.

NORTHWEST FOREST PRODUCTS *(NASDAQ: NWFP)*   Tacoma, WA, 2011–2013
The nation's leading manufacturer and distributor of wood and wood-alternative products; a $2.7B public company

▪ **Account Manager**
Sales of Structural Panels, Construction Lumber & Composite Products | Industrial Accounts | Washington-Oregon Territory

Performed full range of sales, business development, and account management functions including margin accountability, product pricing, proposal development/presentation, order management, and A/R oversight.

	Sales	Margin
Quota	$1.09M	$83K (7.6%)
2012 Results	$1.60M	$145K (9.1%)
Performance to Plan	**147%**	**175%**

- Generated **$700K** in new business for 2 new product lines. Sold more TechTrim than anyone else in the company and won nationwide sales awards for both new products.

STEPHEN X. GORDON   206-561-7612 • sgordon75@gmail.com

SYSTEMS PRODUCTS, INC. *(NYSE: SPI)*   Seattle, WA, 2011–2012
$4.9B global distributor of electronics systems

■ **Sales / New Business Development Representative**
Sales of Wiring Systems & Networking Products | Seattle Region

Developed and qualified prospects, performed needs assessment, worked with technical team to create specifications, presented recommendations, and closed sales. Built customer relationships, providing ongoing account management and maintenance.

- Selected as Sales Specialist for new product focus in digital and closed-circuit security systems Delivered immediate results and long-term contracts, including:
  - King County: **$12K** immediate business and authorization for test installation that resulted in commitment for all future CSU/DSU business.
  - Starbucks: Needs assessment, CCTV demo and test installation, and ultimate capture of **$175K** contract for 58 stores nationwide.
  - Sea-Tac Medical Center: **$130K** contract for networking system for new administration building.
- Identified need, defined solution, and led all aspects of specifying a new access-control system for Tacoma County. First-year revenue projected to be **$250K**, with no-bid follow-on sales for 10 years.

GEORGIA-PACIFIC   Portland, OR, 2004–2011
Second-largest manufacturer of forest products in the US; $2.1B subsidiary of Koch Industries, Inc.

■ **Structural Panels Trader,** 2008–2011
Product Manager for Structural Panels | Building Industry Accounts | 8-State Western Region

- Grew sales **12%** in targeted key accounts.
- Increased gross margin by **32.5%** and maintained highest direct-sales profit of 15 traders in the group.
- Played a key role in advancing group from last to **#3** in sales among 20+ groups nationwide.
- Worked closely with account managers to develop pricing based on market conditions.

■ **Account Manager,** 2006–2008 (40 Accounts | 4-State Territory)
Inside Sales Representative, Salt Lake City, UT, 2004–2006

EDUCATION / ADDITIONAL

B.S. in Management, 2004: University of Washington, Seattle, WA

Sales Training: Quality Sales Skills, Georgia-Pacific

Proficient in MS Word, WordPerfect, Excel, Access, PowerPoint.

Available for travel and relocation.

To: Sylvia Gray, VP Human Resources—XYAN, Inc.
From: Taryn Henshaw
Subject: National Accounts Manager

Dear Ms. Gray:

As National Market Manager with AT&T, I bring to your organization 11 years of progressively responsible experience in the strategic planning, design, and leadership of winning sales and business development programs. My notable achievements include:

- Design of 2 service-driven product extensions and leadership of full-scale market launch. **RESULT: $2M in revenue within first year.**

- Creative concept for the sales strategy for national introduction of a completely new product line. **RESULT: $3.5M in monthly revenue within first year.**

- Innovative idea for bundling commercial services for AT&T's national account portfolio. **RESULT: Consistent wins over the competition AND a measurable improvement in net profitability of each sales transaction.**

Complementing my ability to produce sales dollars are equally strong qualifications in training and leading professional sales teams. Teams and individual performers under my leadership have consistently outperformed sales goals, achieved President's Club distinction, and been promoted to new opportunities.

Your posting indicates that you seek a strong sales performer with decisive and action-driven leadership skills. That is precisely who I am and what I offer to XYAN. May we meet soon?

Sincerely,

Taryn Henshaw
============
Arlington, VA 23068
703-642-4140
taryn.henshaw@gmail.com
LinkedIn.com/in/tarynhenshaw

Keyword Answers to Interview Questions

Tell me about yourself.

Building top-performing sales regions and customer markets is what I do best. Whether launching a new product, developing a new market niche, penetrating a new territory, or revitalizing dormant sales, I have consistently met or exceeded all revenue goals.

With Turner Broadcasting, I increased sales in the Phoenix market by 22% the first year. With Metromedia Broadcasting, I grew sales in the Philadelphia market by 25% the first year, 28% the second year, and 45% the third year. Now, as commercial account sales manager with Paramount Distribution, I am targeting an 18% increase in my first year, after there's been no market increase for the past three years. So, as you can see, I'm a producer who loves to sell, negotiate, and close.

What is the most valuable skill you bring to our company?

Closing the sale is my #1 skill. I can overcome virtually any customer objection and demonstrate the true value of what I'm selling.

I am particularly effective when selling head-to-head against our competition, working just that bit harder to be sure that we get the sale. It is my persistence, thoroughness, and customer relationship style that has driven such significant sales growth in every one of my markets.

What is your most significant achievement?

The revenue increases I delivered while working for Metromedia Broadcasting are some of my most notable achievements. As you may recall in our earlier discussion about the company, I increased sales by 25% in year one, 28% in year two, and 45% in year three.

I was able to revitalize the market, restore customer credibility, capture new accounts, and firmly establish our brand. Then, using a consultative sales process to understand my clients' needs, I positioned Metromedia as the market expert within our industry.

Chapter 24

Teaching and Education

Top 100 Keywords

Academic Advisement

Academic Standards

Academics

Accreditation

Administration

Admissions

Alumni

Assessment Tools

At-Risk Youth

Athletics

Campus Life

Career Counseling

Career Development

Classroom Management

Classroom Teaching

Classroom Technology

Coaching

College

Community College

Community Relations

Conferences

Cooperative Learning

Corporate Training

Course Design

Coursework

Curriculum Development

Differentiated Instruction

Education

Education Administration

Education Management

Educational Psychology

Educational Services

Educational Technology

Enrollment

Externship

Faculty

Field Instruction

Foundation

Grant Administration

Grant Writing

High School

Higher Education

Holistic Learning

Individualized Education
   Program (IEP)

Institutional Effectiveness

Institutional Planning & Research

Instruction

Instructional Media

Instructional Methods

Instructional Technology

Integrated Instruction

Intercollegiate Athletics

Internship

Laboratory

Leadership Development

Learning

Lesson Planning

Lifelong Learning

Literacy

Mainstreaming

Management Development

Multimedia Learning Tools

No Student Left Behind Act

Online Learning

Organizational Development

Parent-Teacher Relations

Peer Counseling

Preschool

Primary School

Private School

Program Development &
   Management

Public & Private Partnerships

Public Education

Public Speaking

Residential Life

Sabbatical

Scholarship

Scholastic Standards

Science, Technology, Engineering
   & Math (STEM)

Secondary School

Seminar

Special Education

Standardized Testing

Student Advisement

Student Counseling

Student Development

Student Management

Student Retention

Student Services

Student Success

Symposium

Teaching

Technology

Textbook Review & Selection

Title 1 Services

Training & Development

Tutoring

University

Web-Based Technology

Workforce Development

Susanna Wu
781-881-1139
susanna.wu@gmail.com

EXPERIENCED ELEMENTARY TEACHER

Shaping reflective, self-directed learners who think critically and creatively.

Energetic and dedicated teacher with a solid foundation in subject matter instruction—particularly science. Experienced with the most up-to-date instructional methodologies, exposed to a variety of collaborative teaching approaches, and skilled at teaching students with wide-ranging capabilities and unique needs.

- Character Education
- Two-year Looping Program
- Differentiated Classroom

- Technology Integration
- Enrichment Programs
- Authentic Assessments

- Diversity Curriculum
- Curriculum Mapping
- Departmentalization

HIGHLIGHTS OF QUALIFICATIONS

→ Experienced with a full range of exceptional children from high-needs remedial students to highly advanced enrichment students. Proven ability to ease the transition of bilingual students into the mainstream school system.

→ Actively engaged in sharing new models of learning and collaborating with other educators to promote innovation and exemplary practices. Continuously seek professional development to expand and reaffirm classroom techniques.

→ Involved in educational improvement initiatives (i.e., Micro Society) that focus on building classroom and school-wide cultures of "thinking" by fostering attitudes, values, and skills that support good critical and creative thinking.

→ Able to recognize and develop students' multiple intellectual strengths, adapting instruction to individual differences, cultural backgrounds, and developmental levels. Also able to assess their work in ways that promote further learning.

→ Possess useful current insights to make sound educational judgments, focus standards, and respond to state frameworks to strengthen teaching and learning of both general education and special education.

TEACHING EXPERIENCE

Malden Public School District, Malden, MA   2010–Present
(Suburban community with a highly diverse and immigrant-rich student population)
Salemwood Elementary School: 5th Grade Teacher—*2013 to Present* ■ **4th Grade Teacher**—*2010–2013*

Shape classroom and instruction materials to help students develop valuable thinking skills and encourage a deeper understanding of concepts within and across disciplines. Develop curriculum marked by diversity of education practices and innovative approaches to learning.

- Rewrote the district's science curriculum and piloted the use of science kits.
- Rewrote the English/Language Arts curriculum to align district program and assessments to state frameworks.
- Yearbook Advisor and Head Coordinator for the annual science fair.
- Coordinator for 5th grade activities, school-wide fairs, and field trips.
- Member of several leadership teams involved with curriculum restructuring.

EDUCATION AND CERTIFICATION

M.S. Elementary Education; Emphasis: Reading
Merrimack University, North Andover, MA

B.A. Social Science and Elementary Education
Salem State University, Salem, MA

Valid Massachusetts Teaching Certificate (Elementary, Grades 1–6)

MARCUS FRENCH

804-388-9090
Reston, VA 24503
marcus.french@gmail.com

January 17, 2016

Dr. Edward Louis, Director
Lincoln School
4930 D Street Northeast
Washington, DC 20046

Dear Dr. Louis:

Thank you for your time on the phone this morning. Our conversation confirmed my interest in a teaching position with the Lincoln School, and I am forwarding my resume as you suggested.

The value and strength that I bring to your school community includes:

- Success teaching across a broad range of learner abilities, customizing each program, course, and curriculum to the individual abilities of each student.

- A unique ability to build camaraderie among students, faculty, administrators, parents, and support personnel. It energizes me to work in an environment where spirit is strong, communication is open, and everyone is focused on success.

- A true, heartfelt commitment to student achievement, as evidenced not only in my teaching ability, but my active involvement in coaching youth sports and athletic programs.

- An extensive background in special events planning, logistics, public relations, and promotions.

Your philosophy of the "optimal match," as described on your website, really resonated with me. In fact, the entire educational concept of the Lincoln School is precisely the foundation upon which my career has flourished. We must nurture each student to academic and personal success. It is the commitment we have made as educators, coaches, and administrators.

I look forward to continuing our discussions. Thank you for your attention and support.

Sincerely,

Marcus French

Keyword Answers to Interview Questions

Tell me about yourself.

I'm your typical elementary school teacher with a most *atypical* approach to classroom management, curriculum development, student learning, and, most importantly, learner retention. I pride myself on my ability to design innovative educational programs that spark my students' interest and encourage them to experience the world.

What's more, I am active throughout the school community, working with the PTA, the media resources committee, the annual fundraising campaign, and the textbook review committee. In addition, I coordinate special event programs, guest speakers, and field trips for the entire elementary school.

What is the most valuable skill you bring to our school?

My most valuable skill is my love for my children. Shouldn't that be at the heart of every teacher? I find tremendous personal and professional satisfaction from watching my children learn.

It is this commitment to my students, along with my outstanding teaching skills, that will make me a valuable and immediate contributor to your school's community, students, teachers, and administrators.

What is your most significant achievement?

Nurturing parental involvement in the classroom is what I consider to be my most notable contribution. When I first came to Rodgers Elementary, none of the parents of my third-grade students ever spent any time at school. So, I launched a plan to encourage my parents to participate in whatever ways possible.

Today I have, at minimum, two parent volunteers in the classroom each day, another group working on the end-of-year celebration, two parents who write and distribute a monthly classroom newsletter, and many other volunteers. Parent involvement has created a truly positive learning environment for all of my students—and the parents love it, too!

Chapter 25

Telecommunications Technology

Top 100 Keywords

Alarm Systems Technology

Architecture

Asynchronous Transfer Mode (ATM)

Automated Call Distribution (ACD) System

Automated Test Tools

Automated Voice Response

Bandwidth

Benchmarking

Broadband

Broadcast Engineering

Business Continuity

Cabling Systems

Call Center Operations

Call Management

Call Routing

Capacity Planning

Cellular Communications

Cloud-based Network Services

Coaxial Cabling

Communications Satellites

Communications Systems

Component Development

Configuration

Data Acquisition Framework

Data Communications

Data Network Engineering

Dense Wave Division Multiplexing (DWDM)

Diagnostics

E-Commerce

E-Trade

Electronic Equipment & Technology

Emerging Technologies

Encryption

Ethernet

Fault Isolation & Analysis

Fiber Optics

Field Engineering

Firewall

Frame Relay

Hardware Engineering

Help Desk

Inbound Call Center

Installation & Maintenance

Internet Protocol (IP) Networking

Legacy Telecommunications
    Systems

Local Area Network (LAN)

Logistics Support

Mobile Broadband

Multi-Platform Integration

Multi-User Interface

Needs Assessment

Network Administration

Network Engineering

Network Operations Center
    (NOC)

Network Routing & Provisioning

Network Service Providers

Network Subnets

Network Systems Design

Network Testing

Next-Generation Technology

Optical Interface

Private Branch Exchange (PBX)

Program Management

Project Lifecycle

Project Management

Project Methodology

Quality Assurance (QA)

Remote Systems Access

Research & Development (R&D)

Root Cause Analysis

Satellite Technology

Secure Networks

Session Initiation Protocol (SIP)

Software Configuration

Software Engineering

Solutions Development & Delivery

Systems Engineering

Systems Integration

Systems Testing

Switch Operations

Synchronous Optical Network
    (SONET)

System Recovery

Technical Documentation

Technical Feasibility Analysis

Telecommunications Engineering

Telecommunications Infrastructure

Telecommunications Solutions

Teleconferencing

Telephony

Troubleshooting

Trunking

Unified Communications (UC)

User Training & Support

Vendor Management

Video Engineering Technology

Voice Over Internet Protocol
    (VOIP)

Voice Programs & Systems   Wide Area Network (WAN)

Voice Solutions   Wireless Communications

NOTE: It is essential that you include your SPECIFIC telecommunications skills (hardware, software, network protocols, etc.) in your resume, along with all of the relevant keywords from the list on the previous pages.

You can include those tech skills in the summary section of your resume, in a separate section titled "Telecommunications Skills," "Telecommunications Technology Qualifications," or "Telecommunications Technology Profile," or you can integrate them into your job descriptions. Without them, your resume will most likely be passed over by electronic keyword scanning systems (also known as ATS technology), so be certain to prominently display them.

STEVEN JAMES

469-329-7843 • stevenjames@gmail.com
www.LinkedIn.com/in/stevenjames

TELECOMMUNICATIONS PROFESSIONAL

10 Years' Progressive Experience with Leading Telecom Companies
Notable Successes in Telecommunications Project Design & Management

CAREER ACHIEVEMENTS

—Project Management—Contractor Management—Productivity & Performance Improvement

- Engineered a contract with a major 17-location account, culminating in accountability as national account contact for all Systimax cabling. **Results:**
  - Upgraded all production/box plants nationwide.
  - Project-managed all locations and sourced nationwide to attain a single point of contact.
  - Delivered finished product that exceeded client expectations and increased future business.

- Spearheaded ground-up construction of a large contractor database (40+ contractors) over a 4-state region to manage business growth. **Results:**
  - **95%** contractor-membership in the Midwest Telecom authorized service program.
  - **35%** climb in company's cabling margin, primarily through analysis/reduction of expenditures.

- Streamlined job bid turnaround time from **1** week to **2–3** days by maximizing technology utilization.

- Slashed accounts receivable process from approximately **8** hours weekly by successfully implementing direct billing method.

—Sales & Marketing—Customer Relationship Management—Team Training

- Exceeded sales quota **175%,** 2 years (Millionaires Club).

- Boosted sales force productivity by training team on key customer questions and methods to identify sales opportunities. **Result:** 50% increase in new business lead generation.

- Achieved **150%** of sales quota, 2 years (Super Achievers Club).

—Leadership & Recognition

- Increased profit margin **25+%;** tagged by ABC Technologies to present success strategies (on generating a profitable cabling business) at wiring conference.

- Nominated by account executives (based on outstanding accomplishments) to attend first ProTel Communications Elite meeting.

- Recruited to Technologies Network Systems National Task Force that originated a pricing structure for Global Emerging Market organization.

STEVEN JAMES
469-329-7843 • stevenjames@gmail.com
Page 2

CAREER PROGRESSION

Steady telecommunications career progression. Began career with National Communications and presently perform project management at TeleSys Communications — each transition generated from company/divisional "spin-offs" (mergers, acquisitions, purchases, etc.).

TeleSys Communications (acquired division of National Communications), Fort Worth, TX, 2012–Present

Regional Wiring Coordinator • Contractor Manager • Provisioning Coordinator

Supervise 40 contractors in 4 states. Plan and execute custom cabling projects from order to installation to billing to customer satisfaction. Participate in design meetings at customer sites. Negotiate with suppliers for optimum material prices and continually streamline processes and procedures, resulting in declining expenses and climbing profits.

Midwest Telecom (spin-off from National Communications), Dallas, TX, 2009–2012

Account Executive • Systems Technician

Consistently exceeded sales quotas, earning placement in Millionaires and Super Achievers Clubs. Originated a profitable cabling business from ground up to 40 contractors in 4 states by effectively networking, accruing leads, generating proposals, and closing sales.

National communications, Dallas, TX, 2006–2009

System Technician • Repair Technician • Installer

EDUCATION / TRAINING / CERTIFICATIONS / KNOWLEDGE

BS in Telecommunications, University of Missouri, Columbia, MO, 2006
Graduate, National Communications Career Path Program, 2008

Certifications: Panduit, Mohawk, Bertek, Belden and ABC Technologies Fiber Optics, SysTel Technologies Systimax Certification in Installation, Sales, and Design/Engineering
Training: LAN and WAN environments, networks, DSU/CSU
Installation/Repair: Tier 1 and Tier 2 Levels

Other: All Comkey Products; AT&T Vintage PBX Switches; Unix Language; Basic/Advanced Electronics

PROFESSIONAL AFFILIATION

Member, BICSI, 2010–Present

Geoff   Travers

geofftravers@hotmail.com   203-546-1234

May 12, 2016

Pamela Highsmith
Client Services Director
Connecticut Telecon, Inc.
119 Asylum Avenue
Hartford, CT 06105

Dear Ms. Highsmith:

Your current posting for a **Video Operations Manager** calls for precisely the skills, experience, leadership, and customer focus I have demonstrated over the past 8 years with Major Telecom.

Consider these highlights of the prime initiatives I have led—and results I've delivered:

- **Technology:** I conceptualized, developed, and implemented a traffic change-over system among global operations centers that cut annual costs by $100K with no reduction in service levels.

- **Operational Efficiency:** Under my leadership, we eliminated 60% of service delivery errors through continuous improvement of systems and processes.

- **Project Management:** One of my proudest successes was planning and implementing the transfer of service for a key global customer—the largest transfer undertaken by my company, completed flawlessly!

- **Customer Support:** By delivering superior customer service, we consistently outshone the competition (a formidable industry leader) and retained 90% of our video operations customers during my tenure.

I guarantee that the strength of my experience and track record of achievement will add measurable value to your organization. I will call you in the next few days to schedule a time to discuss this opportunity and the value I can bring to Connecticut Telecon.

Sincerely,

Geoff Travers

Keyword Answers to Interview Questions

Tell me about yourself.

For the past 12 years, I've helped to design, implement, and manage high-tech call centers for two of the nation's largest banking institutions—Bank of New York and Wells Fargo. Promoted quickly at both companies, I've contributed to the development of more than 10 different call center organizations—both starting up new ventures and turning around operations to achieve aggressive performance, productivity, and profitability milestones.

I find my greatest professional pride comes from my ability to "leave my mark" on every operation that I touch. I'm never satisfied with the status quo; rather, I'm always working to improve how each call center operates, the level of service it provides, the quality of personnel we employ, and, of course, the capabilities of our technologies to meet changing demands. It's been a great career path that I plan to follow for years to come.

What is the most valuable skill you bring to our company?

It's difficult to differentiate the value of my technical experience from my commitment customer service, because they're so interrelated. They are definitely my two strongest skill sets—my understanding of technology and its impact on the business and the bottom line, and my ability to manage high-volume call centers where customer service is the primary benchmark by which we measure our success.

Hand-in-hand with those skills is my ability to train others in both the use of technology and the way we handle customer service calls— from the easy questions to the unhappy customers who may require a good bit of time to restore their confidence in the company. I find great reward in watching those I've trained as they transition from newly hired employees to top-performing associates.

What is your most significant achievement?

My greatest achievement was the transition from outdated technology to the latest generation TriTec solution at Wells Fargo. Working with a team of four others with both technical and leadership experience, we were able to deliver this $2.2 million project three weeks ahead of schedule and right on budget. No one thought it possible … except the five of us, who knew that it was possible … and we proved it.

Chapter 26

Using Keywords in Challenging Job Search Situations

Career Change, Military Transition, Incarceration, Return-to-Work, and Multiple Job Changes

USING KEYWORDS IN YOUR RESUMES, job search letters, LinkedIn profiles, and interview answers can be more difficult for job seekers facing unique employment challenges—those who are:

- Changing from one career, profession, or industry to another

- Transitioning out of the military to related civilian employment

- Moving out of the military and into unrelated civilian employment

- Shifting from incarceration back into society and the world of work

- Returning to work after extended absences (e.g., raising children, illness, caregiving, retirement)

- Best described as "job hoppers" due to frequent job changes

If you fall into any of those categories, keywords are just as important to your job search as they are to everyone else's. And, just like every other job seeker, you want to use keywords that relate to your targeted job search goals—the positions you are currently seeking and not necessarily the jobs you've held in the past, whether that be your current job or a position from 10+ years ago.

As a quick refresher from Chapter 1, keywords fall into five major categories:

- Hard Skills and Factual Data
- Soft Skills and Attributes
- Employment Details
- Education and Training Credentials
- General Information

You can read in detail about each of these on pages 2–4. Taking a few minutes to remember all of the different types of keywords will help as you address your unique job search challenges and situation.

Challenging Situations and Keywords

There is no single keyword list for job seekers in challenging situations. Your most valuable keyword resources are the keyword lists for the industries and professions that you are targeting. As an example, if you're looking for opportunities as an equipment operator in a manufacturing facility, be sure to refer to both Chapter 9 (Equipment Installation, Maintenance, and Repair) and Chapter 17 (Manufacturing and Production Operations).

When reviewing those chapters, identify the keywords that align with the skills, experiences, and educational credentials you have, then incorporate them into all of your career communications and interview answers. Not all of the keywords will be relevant to you or any job seeker, no matter the circumstance, so be sure to review the list(s) closely to find the right keywords for you and your career.

Just as important is the Appendix, where you'll find a list of 221 Personality Descriptors. These keywords are soft skills and essential components for creating a keyword-rich resume. Review the list carefully (pages 174–176) to find your skills and then incorporate them appropriately into your resume, letters, interviews, and all other career messages.

How This Chapter is Structured

To best demonstrate how to use keywords to your advantage, on the following pages we share eight resumes, each of which aligns with one of the special situations listed at the beginning of this chapter. Unlike all of the other profession-specific chapters in this book that include a list of the top 100 keywords and sample resume, cover letter, and interview answers for that profession, this chapter provides you with an explanation of how each of these resumes was written and formatted to best position the candidate for his or her unique job search challenge.

Identify the resume(s) in this chapter that are similar to your situation and review them carefully to understand how they're written, structured, and, most importantly, how the keywords are integrated throughout. Then, refer to the keyword lists in the chapters that relate to the professions you are pursuing, select the keywords that match your skills, and include them prominently in the summary, experience, and education sections of your resume—as appropriate.

Next, refer to the letters in the appropriate chapters throughout this book to help you craft your own winning cover letter. Review the interview answers to help prepare yourself for telephone and in-person interviews.

Keyword Challenge: Career Change

YOUR #1 CHALLENGE: To highlight your skills, qualifications, experiences, achievements, education, and other qualifications that align with your current career goals, while simultaneously downplaying the fact that you're transitioning into a new industry or profession.

Look at David Gregorius's resume on page 151 and you'll see a resume for a job seeker who wants to move from his past career as a retail store manager into a position as an accountant and/or tax specialist. While working as a manager in the retail industry, he's had a lot of accounting and finance responsibilities and also pursued an advanced degree in finance. Based on his objective, these related activities and relevant education become the centerpiece of his entire resume.

Reviewing David's resume, we see:

- It begins with a headline that contains several very important hard skill keywords: Corporate Accounting, Public Accounting, and Taxation.

- Immediately following is an Objective that features a number of important soft skill keywords: Critical Thinking, Creative Problem Solving, Planning, Organization, Analysis.

- As you can see, the Key Skills section is filled with 10 important keywords such as General Accounting, Cost Accounting, Financial and Business Analysis, Risk Management, and MS Office (Word, Excel, Access, PowerPoint).

- The Capabilities—Accounting and Finance section is packed with 20+ relevant keywords: Balance Sheets, Income Statements, GAAP, Capital Budgeting, Valuation, Investment Strategies, and many more.

- Moving on to David's Education section, you'll see that it also has plenty of relevant terms, including his degrees, majors, and all of his relevant coursework. Every one of these is a valuable keyword addition.

DAVID GREGORIUS

davidgregorius@mac.com — 617-962-7835 — LinkedIn.com/in/davidgregorius

CORPORATE ACCOUNTING • PUBLIC ACCOUNTING • TAXATION

OBJECTIVE

Position as Accountant providing opportunity to use knowledge gained through recent education (**MS Accounting and Taxation**) plus strengths demonstrated throughout 8 years in business management: critical thinking, creative problem solving, and excellent planning, organizational, analytical, and financial management skills.

KEY SKILLS

General Accounting ... Cost Accounting ... Financial & Business Analysis ... Asset & Liability Management
Cost & Benefit Analysis ... Financial Modeling ... Auditing ... Risk Assessment ... Working Capital

MS Office (Word, Excel, Access, PowerPoint) ... JD Edwards ... Peachtree Accounting

CAPABILITIES—ACCOUNTING & FINANCE

- Setting up balance sheets, income statements, and cash-flow statements in compliance with GAAP.
- Analyzing financial performance of business operations, tracking and analyzing costs, and creating and implementing cost control systems to achieve corporate objectives.
- Developing and administering budgets; familiar with capital budgeting process. Versed in the different types of corporations, consolidations, and tax advantages.
- Determining valuation of business assets, stock and bond prices, depreciation schedules, and pro-forma statements. Creating capital asset pricing models and financial models.
- Calculating P/E ratios, DCF, EPS, discounted cash flow, and beta for equity security analysis.
- Devising portfolio asset allocation strategies, conducting risk assessments, and developing business plans.
- Designing financial management and investment strategies for both individuals and companies.

EDUCATION

BOSTON COLLEGE, BOSTON, MA
M.S. in Accounting and Taxation, 2016
B.S. in Business Administration with concentration in **Finance,** 2007

Relevant Courses: Advanced Accounting, Intermediate Accounting, Managerial Accounting, Governmental Accounting, Auditing, Finance, Business Law, Cost Accounting, Tax Accounting

BUSINESS MANAGEMENT EXPERIENCE

Manager (2012–Present) / **Assistant Manager** (2008–2012): VALUE STORES, INC., BOSTON, MA

Promoted to manage financial and day-to-day operations of $3M business. Fully accountable for financial functions: auditing financial records, processing payroll, managing cash, balancing drawers, entering inventory on computer system, adjusting inventory retail values, and preparing bank deposits and reconciliations.

Accomplishments

- Improved store's financial performance—from 10% under revenue goal to 3% above revenue goal within the first month as Manager by:
  - Assessing and realigning employee skills with appropriate functions.
  - Improving inventory levels and product mix on sales floor.
  - Reducing turnover, hiring and training high-quality candidates, and implementing a succession plan.
- Boosted profits 20% over prior year, sales by 4% annually, and budgeted profit forecasts by 6% per year.
- Winner of 3 Paragon Awards out of 15 managers in the district for achieving excellence in customer service and exceeding profitability and sales targets. Tapped as mentor to develop and train 25 new store managers.

- Within his Business Management Experience section, the focus is still on the accounting and financial aspects of his retail career, highlighting relevant keywords such as Financial Records, Payroll, Cash, Bank Profits, and Forecasts. You will also notice a few retail industry keywords that round out the resume and give context to the actual job description.

When you look at this resume, you see a qualified accounting and finance professional, which is precisely the goal! What we've done is highlight the keywords related to his objectives while downplaying keywords focused on retail sales and store management.

If you are changing careers, try to avoid the use of the words "transition" or "transfer." You don't want the focus to be on the fact that you're changing from one field to another—with the implication that you don't have a lot of expertise in your new field. Rather, you want the focus to be on what you *do* have—the right skills, knowledge, and qualifications … the right keywords.

COVER LETTER IDEAS: Cover letters and e-notes are always best when written in response to a specific advertisement, job posting, or network contact. However, to give you an idea of what a cover letter for someone in the field of Accounting looks like, read Marcella Koenig's cover letter on page 16. If you're not in Accounting, review the cover letters in this book that relate specifically to your field of work.

Keyword Challenge: Military Transition

YOUR #1 CHALLENGE: To highlight your skills, qualifications, experiences, achievements, education, and more as they relate to your specific career goals—the profession that you're targeting and the types of organizations in which you want to work.

Military transition resumes generally fall into one of three categories:

- Job seekers pursuing similar career paths with companies in defense-related industries and quasi-governmental organizations—companies that will definitely value their military experience.

- Job seekers pursuing similar career paths with commercial companies in industries that are totally unrelated to defense, military, or other similar markets.

- Job seekers pursuing careers in other professions in the commercial and corporate marketplace.

Let's examine each of those possibilities, starting with Aidan O'Hara's resume on page 154. Aidan falls into the first category—a job seeker who wants to continue working in contract administration, procurement, and related functions, just as he's done in his most recent assignment with the US Marine Corps. His goal is to work in government sales and contracting, so keywords in *both* areas are important—those related to his job functions in contracts and those related to his military/government career.

In reviewing Aidan's resume, note the positioning of keywords throughout the entire document:

- The resume begins with a 2-line headline with his most essential hard skill keywords: Government Sales, Contract Administration, Operations Management, Competitive Bidding, E-Procurement, Corporate Security, HR Management.

- The addition of a third subheading line allows him to include details of his very important Top Secret clearance—inevitably one of the essential keywords to be scanned for.

- In the shaded section you see keywords under three relevant headings (Contracts/Bidding/Project Management, Information Management, Team & Operational Leadership) and in each bullet point: Government Bidding Processes, Preferred Vendor Status, Critical Intelligence Information, Security.

- Employment-related keywords are used extensively throughout the Professional Experience section: Executive Officer, Assistant to Director, Major, United States Marine Corps, Joint Intelligence Center, Central Command. These types of keywords are important because companies electronically scan to find resumes for people who've held specific job titles or worked within specific organizations.

- Aidan's Professional Experience section—his most recent position in particular—is flush with relevant keywords: Competitive Bid Contracts, Defense Contractors, RFP, Quality of Bid Response, Intelligence Data, Federal, Command Staff.

- The Education section is straightforward, showcasing his degree and certifications. You'll notice that the abbreviation USMC is used twice. Abbreviations and acronyms are also essential keywords. A company that wants to recruit someone who's transitioning out of the US Armed Forces will likely do a keyword scan for USMC, USAF, USN, and other well-known acronyms and abbreviations.

Now, if your objective is to continue working in the same type of job function but NOT in military/government, all of the keywords related to military, government, defense, and the like are no longer important. Instead, what matters most are keywords that showcase your professional skills and qualifications without much emphasis on the environment (military) where you acquired them. Kyle Robinson's resume on page 155 is a perfect example.

AIDAN O'HARA

Reston, VA 20190 • 703-345-1101 • aidan.ohara@yahoo.com

GOVERNMENT SALES / CONTRACT ADMINISTRATION / OPERATIONS MANAGEMENT
Competitive Bidding • E-Procurement • Corporate Security • HR Management

Top Secret, Secret Compartmented Information (TS/SCI) Clearance

AREAS OF KNOWLEDGE AND EXPERTISE
Contracts / Bidding / Project Management
❖ Managing government bidding processes, evaluating competitive bids, and understanding preferred vendor status on procurement contracts.
❖ Managing customer relationships to ensure needs are met and customer satisfaction is maintained.
❖ Collaborating with IT professionals to develop in-house systems that capitalize on e-procurement opportunities with state and local governments.

Information Management
❖ Establishing and monitoring protocols for controlling access to sensitive information and maintaining security within a large organization.
❖ Compiling and analyzing critical intelligence information in a fast-paced, demanding environment to make both tactical and strategic recommendations to senior decision-makers.

Team & Operational Leadership
❖ Addressing a broad range of HR management issues for organizations with up to 3500 employees; directly supervising up to 80 people.
❖ Managing day-to-day operations of a military unit with full accountability for $10M in capital equipment.

PROFESSIONAL EXPERIENCE

Executive Officer / Assistant to Director (Major)   2012–2016
United States Marine Corps—Assigned to Joint Intelligence Center, Central Command

Managed day-to-day operations of Joint Intelligence Center, including supervising a team of 40 people accountable for analyzing military intelligence data.

- Led the review of competitive bid contracts submitted by defense contractors, ensuring compliance with RFP requirements and analyzing quality of bid response.
- Coordinated the compilation of intelligence data from 30 countries and 10 US Federal agencies.
- Analyzed reliability and accuracy of compiled information and developed proposed action plans.
- Advised senior command staff on tactical and strategic options for engaging high-level targets.

Personnel Manager / Security Officer (2nd Lt. / 1st Lt. / Captain)   2007–2012
United States Marine Corps—Domestic and Foreign Assignments

Completed advanced leadership and technical training, received TS/SCI clearance, and rotated to various field assignments. Deployed to Haiti, Nicaragua, and aboard ship, as well as serving stateside. Provided direct supervision and leadership to up to 80 Marines.

- Served as Security Officer for regiment with 3500 Marines. Monitored access to Top Secret information, took action to control potential leaks, and advised commander on security issues.
- Managed the effective mobilization and utilization of up to $10M in military assets in the field, including weapons systems and military communication systems.

Promoted rapidly through increasingly responsible positions during early career with USMC.   2000–2007

EDUCATION AND PROFESSIONAL DEVELOPMENT

Bachelor of Arts, Political Science—Furman University, Greenville, SC	2000
Certificate in Information Management / Military Intelligence—USMC (Honor Graduate)	2007
Certificate in Leadership—The Basic School—USMC	2006

KYLE ROBINSON

317-356-9205 • kylerobinson@yahoo.com

INVENTORY CONTROL / MANUFACTURING MANAGEMENT

Logistics ... Warehousing ... OSHA ... Production ... Quality ... Training ... Team Leadership

Versatile, proven leader with demonstrated abilities to achieve company goals in cost-effective manner. Procured, supervised, and managed multimillion-dollar inventory. Directed inspection, assembly, quality, and distribution of mission-critical assets worldwide. Skilled in training and developing cross-functional manufacturing teams.

SELECTED ACHIEVEMENTS

▶ **Inventory Control:** Managed company's 615 line-item, **$25M** stock inventory warehouse. Oversaw all inspection, maintenance, warehousing, control and distribution functions. Attained **100%** asset accountability and **99%** warehouse location accuracy for 2015 annual inventory.

▶ **Management:** Directed manufacturing efforts of 85-person team as acting Department Manager. Devised and implemented operational controls to maximize process effectiveness. Ensured consistent on-time delivery and **100%** customer satisfaction.

▶ **Organization:** Authored initial department relocation plans to 4 separate locations involving 70 people and **$4.6M** in equipment assets. Developed detailed operational procedures based on job requirements, staff expertise, and resource availability. Achieved full operational capability in **half** the time planned.

▶ **Training:** Led departmental training program for staff of 85 from 6 work centers. Established master training standards based on job requirements and individual expertise. Implemented precise training guidelines to maintain peak proficiency.

▶ **Quality Assurance:** Oversaw the material procurement, inspection, and manufacture of 500 special, computer-controlled, precision military devices. Designed sound mass-production assembly-line techniques focusing on worker safety and time/motion principles to ensure **100%** product technical accuracy.

▶ **Safety:** Organized and managed department safety program. Performed facility safety inspections and revised and implemented lockout/tag-out program. Increased overall hazard awareness, resulting in **zero** safety mishaps during 3-year tenure.

PROFESSIONAL EXPERIENCE

United States Air Force – Career Highlights   **2005–2016**

Production Superintendent, Minot, ND, 2014–2016
- Maintained high manufacturing standards through efficient procurement of materials and scheduling of workforce.
- Implemented next-generation assembly-line techniques focusing on worker safety and time/motion principles.

Inventory Control & Warehouse Manager, Minot, ND, 2011–2014
- Procured and maintained $25M inventory to support manufacturing efforts.
- Devised document flow plan for shipment of 3500 tons of cargo valued at $10M. Achieved 100% asset accountability.

Operations Control Center Manager, Kadena, Japan, 2008–2011
- Supervised organization scheduling and work monitoring process.
- Coordinated staffing and material support requirements to develop effective work schedules.
- Tracked work-order status, identified constraints, and implemented changes to maintain scheduling effectiveness.

EDUCATION and TRAINING

BS, Business and Management   UNIVERSITY OF MARYLAND, College Park, Maryland, 2015
AS, Systems Technology   AIR FORCE INSTITUTE OF TECHNOLOGY, Wright-Patterson AFB, Ohio, 2006
Organizational Management   USAF SENIOR NCO ACADEMY CORRESPONDENCE COURSE, Kadena AB, Japan, 2010

Kyle wants to continue his career in inventory control, production, operations, and related functions—just as he has done while serving with the USAF. He wants to work in the private sector in a business that has nothing to do with military or defense. Notice how he uses keywords throughout his resume:

- A tightly written headline—Inventory Control and Manufacturing Management—starts his resume and is followed by a second, shaded headline packed full of important keywords: Logistics, Warehousing, OSHA, Production, Quality, Training, Team Leadership.

- The short summary paragraph that follows integrates a nice combination of both soft skill and hard skill keywords, including: Versatile, Cost-Effective, Training, Cross-Functional, Procured, Multimillion-Dollar Inventory, Assembly, Quality, Distribution.

- The Selected Achievements section that follows the summary allows Kyle to fill the top half of his resume with many important keywords and achievements (while never mentioning his military service): Inventory Control, Asset Accountability, Warehouse Location Accuracy, Manufacturing, Operational Controls, On-Time Delivery, Resource Availability, Safety.

- You'll note that his Professional Experience section has only a brief mention of his service with the USAF and uses civilian job titles—Production Superintendent, Inventory Control and Warehouse Manager—rather than focusing on rank or more military-sounding job titles. The content of that section is also written with civilian and corporate keywords—such as Next-Generation Assembly, Time/Motion Principles, Material Support Requirements—that will resonate with his target employers.

- Educational keywords—Kyle's degrees and training—are well positioned for ATS scanning and for the human reader, who can quickly spot those important items.

Our last category for transitioning military personnel encompasses individuals like Diana Lopez, who are both changing careers *and* separating from military service. Diana's resume appears on page 157. If you fall into this category, be certain to read the information here AND the information in the previous section on career change and keywords. Recommendations from both of these sections are important for you.

Here is some basic information about Diana so you'll understand what keywords were highlighted and why. With the USCG for 16 years, she served as an Instructor, Assistant Branch Chief, and Supply Officer. Although the majority of her experience was in supply, operations, and related functions, she did devote about 20% of her time to network administration, and that's where she wants to focus her search. To position her for the jobs she wants, we used a format that emphasizes her *relevant* skills, experiences, and achievements and ends with just a brief mention of her work history.

Diana Lopez

630-555-3626

dianalopez@email.com
www.linked.com/dianalopez

PROFESSIONAL PROFILE

Network Administrator with 10+ years' experience in technical training, project management, computer architecture, and technology operations. Expert in networking, TCP/IP protocol, and network security.

Skilled troubleshooter with attention to detail and ability to work effectively in fast-paced, mission-critical environments. Talented team leader who consistently achieves/surpasses desired results. Top Secret clearance.

TECHNICAL SUMMARY

CERTIFICATIONS

- A+ | Network + | Linux + | LPI | MCSA | CNA
- VMware Certified Professional (VCP)
- Cisco Certified Network Associate, Routing & Switching (CCNA-R&S)

KNOWLEDGE & SKILLS

- Windows 8/10 | Windows 365 | Windows Server 2012 | UNIX | Linux | Exchange Server 2013
- Cisco IOS | TCP/IP | LAN/WAN | BGP | DHCP | DNS | TLS/SSL | Gigabit Ethernet
- VMware vSphere | Data Center & Storage Management Platforms | Cloud Services (SaaS, IaaS, PaaS)

EXPERIENCE HIGHLIGHTS

- **NETWORK ADMINISTRATOR:** Provided workable and proven solutions to support various operating environments. Installed, configured, and maintained the network for military training school, achieving zero classroom downtime for more than 3 years. Demonstrated strong diagnostic abilities with attention to detail and ability to work effectively and efficiently in a high-volume environment.

  Recognized as a competent and credible authority on establishing procedures, conducting tests to verify correct operation of equipment and systems, implementing fault-tolerant procedures for hardware and software failures, and designing audit procedures to test systems integrity and reliability.

- **PROJECT MANAGER:** Managed $3.5M supply inventory and annual budget of $600K. Provided all logistics, including parts issues, contingency purchasing, and emergency field delivery, with no measurable losses.

- **RISK ANALYST:** Identified potential liabilities in computerized military accounting system training program. Analyzed accuracy, usage feasibility, and deficiencies while providing solutions for obstacles.

- **LEADER:** Earned multiple awards for performance excellence. Motivated and inspired organizations ranging in size from 30–400 personnel. Effectively guided and directed associates to achieve their highest potential. Encouraged and supported a teamwork environment that resulted in increased efficiency and productivity.

- **INSTRUCTOR:** Played a major role in design and implementation of self-paced curriculum at military training facility, increasing throughput and retention of more than 150 students per year.

EDUCATION

B.S. Computer Science, Excelsior University, Alameda, CA   2015
A.S. Computer Technology, Empire College, Santa Rosa, CA   2010

EMPLOYMENT

United States Coast Guard   2000–2016

- Supply Officer/Department Head—USCG BOUTWELL (WHEC-719), Alameda, CA, 2010–2015
- Supervisor/Assistant Branch Chief—Maintenance & Logistics Command Pacific, Alameda, CA, 2006–2010
- Instructor—USCG Training Center, Petaluma, CA, 2000–2006

Let's look at Diana's resume to see the keywords and their placement:

- Her Professional Profile section begins with the most important keyword—Network Administrator—the specific job that she's targeting. The two short paragraphs in that section are filled with relevant keywords, such as Technical Training, Project Management, Computer Architecture, Technology Operations, TCP/IP, Network Security.

- That same section also includes important soft skill keywords that will be essential to her search: Troubleshooter, Attention to Detail, Fast-Paced, Mission-Critical, Team Leader.

- The next section—Technical Summary—is an important addition to all job seekers (military and civilian) with hands-on tech responsibilities. These technology skills include many of the primary keywords a company will use to scan for new candidates—terms such as A+, CNA, Cisco Certified Network Administrator, Routing and Switching.

- The Experience Highlights section allows us to bring Diana's relevant roles to the forefront of the resume and not bury them within the job descriptions—under job titles that have almost no correlation with the tasks, responsibilities, and projects she wants to highlight. The first section—Network Administrator—is two paragraphs that are rich with keywords for networking and related functions: Operating Environments, Diagnostic Abilities, Fault-Tolerant Procedures, Hardware and Software, Test Systems Integrity.

- Education focuses exclusively on her two degrees: Computer Science (just attained) and Computer Technology.

- The final section—Employment—does not contain any relevant keywords to support her current search and job targets. It is included just to explain where she has worked and progressed.

COVER LETTER IDEAS: Cover letters and e-notes are always best when written in response to a specific advertisement, job posting, or network contact. However, to give you an idea of what cover letters for job seekers in the fields of Purchasing, Manufacturing, and Telecommunications look like, be sure to read these cover letters: Dana Whitehouse (page 118), Chris Chandler (page 101), and Geoff Travers (page 146). If you're not in any of those professions, review the cover letters in this book that relate specifically to your field of work.

Keyword Challenge: Ex-Offenders

YOUR #1 CHALLENGE: To focus on your skills and any related work experience or education that supports your current job goals.

For a great example of an ex-offender resume for someone with limited work experience, see Cory English's resume on page 160. When you review his work experience section that's near the bottom of the page, you'll see that he has worked at several restaurants. In fact, his most recent job—Kitchen Worker with the State of New York—was during his incarceration!

Note how his important keywords have been integrated into the resume:

- The objective statement—Breakfast and Lunch Cook—puts those important keywords (also known as job titles)—at the forefront of his resume. The remainder of his objective includes other hard and soft skill keywords, such as Restaurant, Customer Base, Culinary Arts, Strong Work Ethic.

- His Personal Profile section focuses almost entirely on the soft skills that make him a valuable candidate: Critical Thinking, Problem Solving, Team Player, Dependable, Hardworking. And his bilingual language skills, a big plus, are also prominently positioned.

- Cooking Skills follow, and you'll see that section is packed with keywords: Entrees, Food Preparation, Service, Safety, Inventory, Tableware, Meats, Baked Goods, Food Preparation, Cooking.

- Cory's job titles, also important for their keyword value, are prominently displayed in bold for both electronic scans and human eyes: Kitchen Worker, Short Order Cook, Prep Cook, Lunch and Dinner Cook.

- Military Service adds a nice bonus to this resume, particularly because his honorable discharge attests to the quality of his work and his character.

- Because his only education is a GED, which he obtained in the service, it's an important addition to that section. Many companies will require a GED and will use that as a primary keyword for scanning to identify qualified candidates.

The second ex-offender resume we've included is for Taylor Grandison on page 161. To understand this resume, know that Taylor was incarcerated as a young adult and had no prior work or educational experience. She's used her time wisely while in prison and is now pursing her first professional job as a Dental Assistant.

CORY ENGLISH

387-458-3241   ⌅ coryenglish@yahoo.com

OBJECTIVE

BREAKFAST and LUNCH COOK

To assist a restaurant in attracting and retaining a strong customer base,
by applying a passion for the culinary arts and a strong work ethic.

PERSONAL PROFILE

Experienced working in a kitchen environment, filling orders, and developing menu items.

Able to get the job done by employing critical-thinking and problem-solving skills.

Work well as a team player and independently with very little supervision.

Received commendations for being dependable and hardworking.

Bilingual, Spanish and English.

COOKING SKILLS

☑ Prepared a selection of entrees, vegetables, desserts, and refreshments.

☑ Cleaned the grill, food preparation surfaces, counters, and floors.

☑ Met quality standards for food preparation, service, and safety.

☑ Trained and supervised workers.

☑ Maintained inventory logs and placed orders to replenish stocks of tableware, linens, paper, cleaning supplies, cooking utensils, food, and beverages.

☑ Received and checked the content of deliveries and evaluated the quality of meats, poultry, fish, vegetables, and baked goods.

☑ Oversaw food preparation and cooking.

WORK EXPERIENCE

Kitchen Worker — State of New York, Coxsackie, NY
Short Order Cook — Rockies Breakfast Bar, Rochester, NY
Prep Cook/Laborer — New World Diner, Rochester, NY
Lunch and Dinner Cook — Albany's Italian American Restaurant, Albany, NY

MILITARY SERVICE

US Navy — Machinist Mate E-3 — *Honorable Discharge*

GED obtained

Taylor Grandison

Greenville, SC
864-888-2482 • taylorgrandison@yahoo.com

PROFILE

A motivated, quality-oriented professional with a solid base of career preparation and training as a Dental Assistant: familiarity with dental procedures, chair-side techniques, and office skills, and a commitment to provide quality dental care and services.

CREDENTIALS

• DENTAL ASSISTANT CERTIFICATION   • RADIOGRAPHY (X-RAY) CERTIFICATION

EDUCATION

DENTAL ASSISTING CERTIFICATE, *State of South Carolina Vocational Training Program*   2016
Successfully completed intensive 6-month program.

Areas of Study:

• General Dentistry • Periodontics • Orthodontics • Endodontics • Pediatric Dentistry
• Oral and Maxillofacial Surgery • Oral Pathology • Fixed and Removable Prostodontics
• Pain Management / Anxiety • Chair-Side Restorative Materials • Pharmacology • Sterilization
• Office / Clerical Functions: Business Management / Administration • Ethics and Jurisprudence

RADIOGRAPHY TRAINING, *State of South Carolina Vocational Training Program*   2015

DENTAL LABORATORY EXPERIENCE

• Alginate Impressions • Pouring / Trimming Models • Preparing Whitening Trays and Provisionals
• Acrylic Resin Custom Trays • Bite Registrations • Polysulfide Impressions • Fluoride Application
• Adapting, Trimming and Seating Custom Temporary Restorations • Placement of Dental Dams

DENTAL INTERNSHIP

DENTAL ASSISTANT INTERN, *Dr. David Jones*   2015–2016
Chair-Side Assistant for dental surgeries.

Experience:

• Composites • Extractions • Sealants • Amalgams • Radiographs (X-Ray)
• Seated Stainless Steel Crowns • Assembly of Tofflemire Matrix Bands
• Implants • Bindings • X-Rays • Sterilization • Patient Charting
• Patient Education in Total Dental Care and Preventive Maintenance

EMPLOYMENT EXPERIENCE

HEALTH CENTER CLERK, *State of South Carolina*   2013–2016

Receptionist: Scheduled appointments and greeted patients.

Records Manager: Maintained confidentiality and accuracy in updating charts and filing information. Ensured adherence to regulatory standards and guidelines, including HIPAA (Health Insurance Portability and Accountability Act).

Physician Attendant: Prepared examination rooms and equipment. Assisted doctors in administering health care treatments and procedures.

Let's see how keywords were used to her advantage:

- The Profile section at the beginning of the resume instantly positions her to meet her job targets by including important keywords: Dental Assistant, Dental Procedures, Chair-Side Techniques, Quality Dental Care.

- Certifications always validate an individual's area of expertise, and Taylor's two credentials immediately follow the Profile to verify her qualifications.

- The Education section includes a brief mention of both of her training programs and then a comprehensive list of keywords (Areas of Study) that include General Dentistry, Periodontics, Orthodontics, Endodontics, Pediatric Dentistry, Oral and Maxillofacial Surgery.

- The next two sections—Dental Laboratory Experience and Dental Internship— are also essential and packed full of keywords that summarize the vast amount of hands-on experience she's acquired, everything from Pouring Molds to Patient Charting.

- The final section on Taylor's resume—Employment Experience—contains important keywords from many keyword categories such as Employment Details (job titles) as well as the hard skills required in each position: Appointments, Patients, Confidentiality, HIPAA, Regulatory Standards, Examination Rooms.

COVER LETTER IDEAS: Cover letters and e-notes are always best when written in response to a specific advertisement, job posting, or network contact. However, to give you an idea of what a cover letter for someone in the field of Hospitality looks like, read Thomas Washington's cover letter on page 78. If you're not in Hospitality, review the cover letters in this book that relate specifically to your field of work.

Keyword Challenge: Return to Work

YOUR #1 CHALLENGE: To prominently display all of your relevant skills, qualifications, experiences, achievements, education, and more, while drawing attention AWAY from the fact that you may not have worked for some time.

This category represents moms and dads returning to work after raising children, people returning to work after an illness or a period of time as a caregiver, people rejoining the workforce after retirement, and anyone else who has decided to re-enter the job market. The challenge is to leverage keywords that relate to current career goals in such as way as to focus on those qualifications while minimizing attention to the fact that the person has been out of the workforce for a period of time.

Allison Henry's resume on page 164 is a great example of a return-to-work mom who's been raising children for the past seven years. Not interested in returning to the real estate or construction industries, she would rather use her strong business and office management skills in a different type of company or position. Here's how we used keywords to her advantage in her resume:

- The two-line keyword headline says it all in terms of positioning her for her target jobs: Business Support Specialist ... Go-to resource with strong problem-solving skills and a flair for client relations. It's a nice blend of both hard skills and soft skills.

- The paragraph that starts the summary section is filled with important soft skill keywords, including Organized, Efficient, Follow-Through, Communicator, Self-Starter.

- Key Strengths, a sub-section within the summary, provides three columns of keywords and keyword phrases, all of which are important for her targeted job in business support and office management.

- To best highlight her experience, Select Accomplishments position this information prominently. Each of the four parts of this section focuses on a different set of essential keywords: Multiple Projects and Administrative Details, Excellence in Customer Service, Mastery of New Tasks to Improve Office Effectiveness, and New Process and Procedure Setup. Then, within each sub-section are three specific achievements written to be rich in keywords.

- Allison's Professional Experience section is deliberately kept to a minimum in an effort to focus on Employment Detail keywords: most significantly, her job titles, which align with her current goals. Dates are somewhat hidden so as to not draw attention to them, and employers are listed without details.

- You'll note that her degree in Secretarial Science is the first entry under Education so that it's seen by both electronic scanners and human eyes to pick up that valuable keyword language.

ALLISON HENRY

Baltimore, MD 21220 ◆ 410-559-9862 ◆ allisonhenry@gmail.com

BUSINESS SUPPORT SPECIALIST

Go-to resource with strong problem-solving skills and a flair for client relations

Well-regarded support professional with a record of success in overseeing administrative processes and coordinating programs in support of business goals. Organized, effective multi-tasker known for persistent approach, thorough follow-through, and calmness under pressure. Persuasive communicator who is effective in developing rapport with others while building trust and respect. Disciplined self-starter who can be relied on to get the job done no matter what the challenge.

Key Strengths:

◆ Project Coordination	◆ Research & Reporting	◆ Record Keeping
◆ Process Management	◆ Problem-Solving	◆ Billing & nvoicing
◆ MS Word & Excel	◆ Customer Service	◆ Accounting & QuickBooks

SELECT ACCOMPLISHMENTS

➤ **Coordinated multiple projects, managing all administrative details for as many as 15 property listings at a time.**
  ▷ Processed files and coordinated preparation of marketing materials to get new listings into system.
  ▷ Worked closely with attorney offices, mortgage companies, home inspectors, and clients, serving as liaison to expedite transactions and facilitate the sales process.
  ▷ Recognized by manager for hastening sales by maintaining open communication and keeping projects on track.

➤ **Reliably delivered excellent service, applying on-target customer service instincts and keen attention to detail.**
  ▷ Implemented communication plan to keep clients informed of sale progress and alert them to next steps.
  ▷ Earned praise from clients for providing service levels that went above and beyond industry standards.
  ▷ Diligently followed up on all details, providing advice and insights to ensure a smooth process for clients.

➤ **Quickly mastered new processes and procedures and served as resource to others to improve office effectiveness.**
  ▷ Provided computer training to new office personnel to help them get up to speed on new systems.
  ▷ Updated and maintained office listing that compiled contact information for business resources (mortgage companies, attorneys, home inspectors, etc.) for recommendation to clients.
  ▷ Reviewed, edited, and approved content for brochures and website.

➤ **Set up and managed all administrative processes and procedures for small business.**
  ▷ Implemented QuickBooks to improve ease and accuracy of record keeping and accounting.
  ▷ Cultivated and maintained strong relationships with supply companies.
  ▷ Provided timely, accurate invoicing and bill-paying services.

PROFESSIONAL EXPERIENCE

Administrative Assistant & Sales Agent, 2006–2009—LORD CALVERT REALTY
Sales Agent, 2003–2006—FELLS POINT REALTY
Office Manager, 2001–2003—COASTAL CONSTRUCTION

EDUCATION & LICENSURE

A.S., Secretarial Science, Prince George's County Community College
Licensed Real Estate Agent (Maryland)

VOLUNTEER ACTIVITIES

Fundraising Volunteer, Girls on the Run of Baltimore (supporting girls in athletics)
Corporate Volunteer, Crab Festival (representing Lord Calvert Realty)
Vice President, Towson High School Football Booster Club
Volunteer, Silver Springs Community Day

COVER LETTER IDEAS: Cover letters and e-notes are always best when written in response to a specific advertisement, job posting, or network contact. However, to give you an idea of what a cover letter for someone in the field of Administration looks like, read Michael Rodriguez's cover letter on page 22. If you're not in Administration, review the cover letters in this book that relate specifically to your field of work.

Keyword Challenge: Job Hopping

YOUR #1 CHALLENGE: To prominently display all of your relevant skills, qualifications, experiences, achievements, education, and more, while drawing attention AWAY from the fact that you've held quite a number of different jobs, many for short periods.

Tanya Dickerson's resume on page 166 demonstrates an effective strategy to make work experience appear to be more stable than it actually was. The keywords are an all-important part of this resume, but so is the structure of her work experience. You'll note that her resume lists all of her jobs together, under the single heading of Staff RN (2005–2016). That shows an 11-year tenure of work, and the fact that her employment was at multiple hospitals and health centers seems almost irrelevant. Great positioning for a job hopper!

Now, let's see how Tanya's keywords work for her:

- The keywords in her headline—Staff Nurse—Permanent / Floating / Shift Work— clearly communicate who she is and the types of opportunities she is pursuing.

- Her Professional Profile section integrates both hard and soft skills that are valuable for anyone in the nursing and health care fields: Empathetic, High-Quality Care, Healing, Pain Management, Healthcare Team, Flexibility. And, to further strengthen that section, additional keywords highlighted in bold print at the end add value to her candidacy.

- In the Experience section, where her jobs are all integrated under the singular Staff RN heading, you will find a large number of keywords related to both patient care and specific medical disciplines. Both sets of keywords make this section rank very high in keyword richness.

- The Education and Training section focuses on her nursing degree and other medical training, all very important for the keyword scanning process.

Tanya Dickerson, BSN

Camden, AR 71701 • 501-380.6011 • tanyadickerson@yahoo.com

PROFESSIONAL PROFILE

STAFF NURSE — PERMANENT / FLOATING / SHIFT WORK

- Empathetic and intuitive in patient interactions; committed to providing high-quality care as an essential link in healing and pain management.
- Poised and confident contributing member of the healthcare team.
- Flexible in quickly mastering new terms, technologies, and systems.
- Demonstrated flexibility and resourcefulness in adapting to ever-changing complexity in the healthcare industry.

Medical Terminology • Medical Procedures • Healthcare Services • Medical Care • Insurance • Inventory/Ordering

EXPERIENCE

Staff RN • 2005–2016

HURON VALLEY OUTPATIENT SURGERY CENTER, Camden, AR
COMANCHE HEALTH CENTER, El Dorado, AR
SOUTHERN MEDICAL CENTER, Camden, AR
SOUTH CENTRAL HEALTH SERVICES, Crossett, AR

- Promoted patient health through a comprehensive range of healthcare services.
- Identified patient care requirements; established a compassionate environment; assured quality of care; resolved patient problems and needs; protected patient and employee rights; documented patient care services; fostered continuity among nursing/physician/therapist teams
- Maintained medical supply inventory.
- Kept updated on professional and technical knowledge.
- Maintained cooperative relationships with healthcare teams and contributed to team effort.
- Managed duties in both scrubbing and circulating for multi-specialty cases, including general, orthopedic, cardiovascular, ophthalmic, gynecologic, plastic, and urologic.
- Member of Trauma Team; dealt with life-threatening surgical cases and critical medical conditions requiring surgical intervention.
- Managed orthopedic department (equipment, supplies); oversaw orthopedic cases throughout medical procedures.

EDUCATION & TRAINING

VATTEROTT COLLEGE, Joplin, MO
Bachelor of Science Degree in Nursing • 2005

Numerous in-service classes and medical-related courses

OTHER INFORMATION

Active in:

- School activities—room parent, lunch aide, member of several committees.
- Church committees—involved with various special events and programs.

COVER LETTER IDEAS: Cover letters and e-notes are always best when written in response to a specific advertisement, job posting, or network contact. However, to give you an idea of what a cover letter for someone in the field of Health Care looks like, read Leslie Silverman's cover letter on page 73. If you're not in Health Care, review the cover letters in this book that relate specifically to your field of work.

Summary

In this chapter, we've addressed a number of challenging job search situations and circumstances and demonstrated how different job seekers used keywords to their advantage. Whatever career challenge you're facing, we're certain that bits and pieces of each section will help you to find the best way to integrate the right keywords to meet your job targets and professional goals.

Appendix

IN THIS APPENDIX, you'll find two very useful tools to help you write and communicate with power:

- List of 425 Resume Writing Verbs
- List of 221 Personality Descriptors

You can use these words in your resume, cover letters, thank-you letters, LinkedIn profiles, interview answers, and all of your other job search communications.

Use them wisely, as each word communicates a unique message that can be valuable in positioning you for success in your job search campaign and lifelong career.

Resume Writing Verbs

Long gone are the days when you'd write a resume, cover letter, LinkedIn profile, or any other job search document that was filled with phrases such as "Responsible for" or "Duties included"—terms that mean nothing.

Today's modern job search documents should be filled with verbs that quickly communicate a message of power and ownership of all that you've done and accomplished.

Use this list of 425 verbs to write with verve and make your career communications come alive!

Accelerate	Assemble	Classify
Accentuate	Assess	Close
Accommodate	Assist	Coach
Accomplish	Attain	Cobble
Achieve	Augment	Collaborate
Acquire	Authenticate	Collect
Adapt	Author	Command
Address	Authorize	Commercialize
Adjudicate	Balance	Commoditize
Administer	Believe	Communicate
Advance	Bestow	Compare
Advise	Brainstorm	Compel
Advocate	Brief	Compile
Align	Budget	Complete
Alter	Build	Comply
Analyze	Calculate	Compute
Anchor	Capitalize	Conceive
Apply	Capture	Conceptualize
Appoint	Catalog	Conclude
Appreciate	Catapult	Conduct
Arbitrate	Centralize	Configure
Architect	Champion	Conserve
Arrange	Change	Consolidate
Articulate	Chart	Construct
Ascertain	Clarify	Consult

Contemporize
Continue
Contract
Control
Convert
Convey
Coordinate
Correct
Corroborate
Counsel
Craft
Create
Critique
Crystallize
Curtail
Cut
Decipher
Decrease
Define
Delegate
Deliver
Demonstrate
Deploy
Derive
Design
Detail
Detect
Determine
Develop
Devise
Differentiate
Diminish
Direct
Discard
Discern

Discover
Dispense
Display
Distinguish
Distribute
Diversify
Divert
Document
Dominate
Double
Draft
Drive
Earn
Edit
Educate
Effect
Effectuate
Elect
Elevate
Eliminate
Emphasize
Empower
Enact
Encourage
Endeavor
Endorse
Endure
Energize
Enforce
Engineer
Enhance
Enlist
Enliven
Ensure
Entrench

Equalize
Eradicate
Espouse
Establish
Estimate
Evaluate
Examine
Exceed
Excel
Execute
Exhibit
Exhort
Expand
Expedite
Experiment
Explode
Explore
Export
Extract
Extricate
Facilitate
Finalize
Finance
Follow up
Forecast
Forge
Form
Formalize
Formulate
Foster
Found
Fulfill
Gain
Garner
Generate

Govern	Judge	Network
Graduate	Justify	Nominate
Guide	Land	Normalize
Halt	Launch	Obfuscate
Handle	Lead	Obliterate
Head	Lecture	Observe
Helmed	Leverage	Obtain
Hire	Liaise	Offer
Honor	License	Officiate
Hypothesize	Listen	Operate
Identify	Locate	Optimize
Illustrate	Lower	Orchestrate
Imagine	Maintain	Order
Implement	Manage	Organize
Import	Manipulate	Orient
Improve	Manufacture	Originate
Improvise	Map	Outpace
Increase	Market	Outperform
Influence	Marshall	Outsource
Inform	Master	Overcome
Initiate	Mastermind	Overhaul
Innovate	Maximize	Oversee
Inspect	Measure	Participate
Inspire	Mediate	Partner
Install	Mentor	Perceive
Institute	Merge	Perfect
Instruct	Minimize	Perform
Integrate	Model	Persuade
Intensify	Moderate	Pilot
Interpret	Modify	Pinpoint
Interview	Monetize	Pioneer
Introduce	Monitor	Plan
Invent	Motivate	Position
Inventory	Navigate	Predict
Investigate	Negotiate	Prepare

Prescribe	Record	Salvage
Present	Recruit	Sanctify
Preside	Rectify	Satisfy
Prevent	Recycle	Save
Process	Redefine	Schedule
Procure	Redesign	Secure
Produce	Reduce	Select
Program	Reengineer	Separate
Progress	Regain	Serve
Project	Regulate	Service
Project manage	Rehabilitate	Set up
Proliferate	Reimagine	Shepherd
Promote	Reinforce	Simplify
Propel	Rejuvenate	Slash
Propose	Relate	Sold
Prospect	Remedy	Solidify
Prove	Render	Solve
Provide	Renegotiate	Spark
Publicize	Renew	Speak
Purchase	Renovate	Spearhead
Purify	Reorganize	Specialize
Qualify	Report	Specify
Quantify	Reposition	Standardize
Query	Represent	Steer
Question	Research	Stimulate
Raise	Resolve	Strategize
Rate	Respond	Streamline
Ratify	Restore	Strengthen
Realign	Restructure	Structure
Rebuild	Retain	Study
Recapture	Retrieve	Substantiate
Receive	Reuse	Succeed
Recognize	Review	Suggest
Recommend	Revise	Summarize
Reconcile	Revitalize	Supervise

Supplement	Test	Unite
Supply	Thwart	Update
Support	Train	Upgrade
Surpass	Transcribe	Use
Synergize	Transfer	Utilize
Synthesize	Transform	Validate
Systematize	Transition	Verbalize
Tabulate	Translate	Verify
Tailor	Trim	Win
Target	Troubleshoot	Work
Teach	Uncover	Write
Terminate	Unify	

Personality Descriptors

Personality descriptors—also known as soft skills—are a valuable addition to your resume, cover letters, LinkedIn profiles, and other career communications, as well as all of your interviews. Peruse the following 221 descriptors and integrate them, as appropriate, to demonstrate that you bring the personal talents that companies and recruiters are seeking in qualified candidates.

Abstract	Cross-Cultural	Entrepreneurial
Accurate	Culturally Conscious	Ethical
Action-Driven	Culturally Sensitive	Experienced
Adaptable	Customer-Driven	Expert
Adventurous	Dauntless	Expressive
Aggressive	Decisive	Flexible
Agile	Dedicated	Focused
Amenable	Dependable	Forward-Thinking
Analytical	Detail-Oriented	Global
Artful	Determined	Go-Getter
Assertive	Devoted	Hardworking
Believable	Diligent	Healthy
Bilingual	Diplomatic	Helpful
Bold	Direct	Heroic
Brave	Dramatic	High-Impact
Capable	Driven	High-Potential
Collaborative	Dynamic	Honest
Communicative	Eager	Honorable
Competent	Earnest	Humanistic
Competitive	Effective	Humanitarian
Conceptual	Efficient	Humorous
Confident	Eloquent	Immediate
Conscientious	Employee-Driven	Impactful
Conservative	Empowered	Important
Consistent	Encouraging	Impressive
Cooperative	Energetic	Incomparable
Courageous	Energized	Individualistic
Creative	Enterprising	Independent
Credible	Enthusiastic	Industrious

Ingenious
Innovative
Insightful
Intelligent
Intense
Intuitive
Investigative
Judicious
Keen
Leader
Loyal
Managerial
Market-Driven
Masterful
Mature
Mechanical
Methodical
Mindful
Modern
Moral
Motivated
Motivational
Multilingual
Notable
Noteworthy
Objective
Observant
Opportunistic
Oratorical
Orderly
Organized
Outstanding
Participative
Participatory
Passionate
Peerless

Perfectionist
Performance-Driven
Persevering
Persistent
Personable
Persuasive
Philosophical
Photogenic
Pioneering
Poised
Polished
Popular
Positive
Practical
Pragmatic
Precise
Preeminent
Prepared
Proactive
Problem-Solver
Productive
Professional
Proficient
Progressive
Prominent
Prompt
Prudent
Punctual
Quality-Driven
Quick Learner
Reactive
Reliable
Reputable
Resilient
Resourceful
Respectful

Responsive
Results-Driven
Results-Oriented
Savvy
Selfless
Sensitive
Sharp
Skilled
Skillful
Sophisticated
Specialist
Spirited
Strategic
Strong
Subjective
Successful
Tactful
Tactical
Talented
Task-Oriented
Teacher
Team Builder
Team Leader
Team Player
Technical
Tenacious
Thorough
Timely
Tolerant
Top Performer
Top Producer
Traditional
Trainer
Transformative
Trilingual
Troubleshooter

Trustworthy

Truthful

Understanding

Unifying

Unrelenting

Up-To-Date

Upbeat

Valiant

Valuable

Venturesome

Veracious

Verbal

Victorious

Vigorous

Virtuous

Visionary

Vital

Vivacious

Well-Balanced

Well-Versed

Winning

Wise

Worldly

Youthful

Zealous

Zestful

Career Resources

THE FOLLOWING CAREER resources are available from Impact Publications. Full descriptions of each, as well as downloadable catalogs and video clips, can be found at www.impact publications. com. Complete the following form or list the titles, include shipping (see formula at the end), enclose payment, and send your order to:

IMPACT PUBLICATIONS
9104 Manassas Drive, Suite N
Manassas Park, VA 20111-5211
1-800-361-1055 (orders only)
Tel. 703-361-7300 or Fax 703-335-9486
Email: query@impactpublications.com
Quick & easy online ordering: www.impactpublications.com

Orders from individuals must be prepaid by check, money order, or major credit card. Since prices may change, please verify online at www.impactpublications.com before ordering. We accept telephone, fax, and email orders. Some titles available on GSA Schedule.

QTY.	TITLES	PRICE	TOTAL
Featured Title (GSA Schedule – Contract #GS-02F-0146X)			
_____	The Best Keywords for Resumes, Letters, and Interviews	$19.95	_____
Other Books by Authors			
_____	The $100,000+ Entrepreneur	$19.95	_____
_____	The $100,000+ Job Interview	19.95	_____
_____	Best Career Transition Resumes for $100,000+ Jobs	24.95	_____
_____	Best Resumes for College Students and New Grads	16.95	_____
_____	Best Resumes and CVs for International Jobs	24.95	_____
_____	Best Resumes and Letters for Ex-Offenders	19.95	_____
_____	Best Resumes for $100,000+ Jobs	24.95	_____
_____	Best Resumes for People Without a Four-Year Degree	19.95	_____
_____	Executive Job Search for $100,000 to $1 Million+ Jobs	24.95	_____
_____	Expert Resumes for Military-to-Civilian Transitions	18.95	_____
_____	KeyWords to Nail Your Job Interview	17.95	_____
_____	Modernize Your Resume	18.95	_____
Pocket Guides (GSA Schedule – Contract #GS-02F-0146X)			
_____	Anger Management Pocket Guide	$2.95	_____
_____	Military Personal Finance Pocket Guide	2.95	_____
_____	Military Spouse's Employment Pocket Guide	2.95	_____
_____	Military-to-Civilian Transition Pocket Guide	2.95	_____
_____	Quick Job Finding Pocket Guide	2.95	_____
_____	Re-Entry Employment & Life Skills Pocket Guide	2.95	_____
_____	Re-Entry Personal Finance Pocket Guide	2.95	_____
_____	Re-Entry Start-Up Pocket Guide	2.95	_____
_____	Re-Imagining Life on the Outside Pocket Guide	2.95	_____
Career Exploration			
_____	50 Best Jobs for Your Personality	$19.95	_____
_____	100 Great Jobs and How to Get Them	17.95	_____
_____	150 Best Jobs for a Secure Future	17.95	_____
_____	150 Best Jobs for Your Skills	17.95	_____
_____	200 Best Jobs for Introverts	16.95	_____

QTY.	TITLES	PRICE	TOTAL
_____	200 Best Jobs Through Apprenticeships	24.95	_____
_____	250 Best-Paying Jobs	17.95	_____
_____	300 Best Jobs Without a Four-Year Degree	20.95	_____
_____	America's Top Jobs for People Re-Entering the Workforce	17.95	_____
_____	Best Jobs for the 21st Century	19.95	_____
_____	Career Guide for Creative and Unconventional People	14.99	_____
_____	Compassionate Careers	16.99	_____
_____	Occupational Outlook Handbook	19.95	_____
_____	Progressive Careers	229.95	_____
_____	Top 100 Health-Care Careers	25.95	_____

Finding Jobs and Getting Hired

QTY.	TITLES	PRICE	TOTAL
_____	The 2-Hour Job Search	$12.99	_____
_____	95 Mistakes Jobs Seekers Make...and How to Avoid Them	13.95	_____
_____	Career Playbook	14.00	_____
_____	Change Your Job, Change Your Life	21.95	_____
_____	Encore Career Handbook	16.95	_____
_____	Getting a Job You Want After 50 For Dummies	22.99	_____
_____	Guerrilla Marketing for Job Hunters 3.0	21.95	_____
_____	Job Hunting Tips for People With Hot and Not-So-Hot Backgrounds	17.95	_____
_____	Knock 'Em Dead: The Ultimate Job Search Guide	16.99	_____
_____	No One Will Hire Me!	15.95	_____
_____	Overcoming Employment Barriers	19.95	_____
_____	The Quick 30/30 Job Solution	14.95	_____
_____	Second-Act Careers	14.99	_____
_____	What Color is Your Parachute? (annual edition)	19.99	_____

Career Assessment

QTY.	TITLES	PRICE	TOTAL
_____	Career Match	$15.00	_____
_____	Discover What You're Best At	15.99	_____
_____	Do What You Are	18.99	_____
_____	Everything Career Tests Book	15.99	_____
_____	Gifts Differing	18.95	_____
_____	Go Put Your Strengths to Work	16.00	_____
_____	I Don't Know What I Want, But I Know It's Not This	15.00	_____
_____	Pathfinder	17.95	_____
_____	What Color Is Your Parachute Workbook	12.99	_____
_____	What Should I Do With My Life?	18.00	_____
_____	What Type Am I?	17.00	_____
_____	What You're Really Meant to Do	25.00	_____

Assessment Instruments (packages of 25)

QTY.	TITLES	PRICE	TOTAL
_____	Barriers to Employment Success Inventory	$63.95	_____
_____	Career Exploration Inventory	60.95	_____
_____	Job Survival and Success Scale	53.95	_____
_____	Transition-to-Work Inventory	57.95	_____

Resumes and Cover Letters

QTY.	TITLES	PRICE	TOTAL
_____	101 Best Resumes	$20.00	_____
_____	201 Dynamite Job Search Letters	19.95	_____
_____	Blue-Collar Resume and Job Hunting Guide	15.95	_____

QTY.	TITLES	PRICE	TOTAL
_____	Damn Good Resume Guide	11.99	_____
_____	Gallery of Best Resumes for People Without a Four-Year Degree	18.95	_____
_____	Haldane's Best Cover Letters for Professionals	15.95	_____
_____	Haldane's Best Resumes for Professionals	15.95	_____
_____	High Impact Resumes and Letters	19.95	_____
_____	Knock 'Em Dead Cover Letters	14.99	_____
_____	Knock 'Em Dead Resumes	14.99	_____
_____	Military-to-Civilian Resumes and Letters	21.95	_____
_____	Nail the Cover Letter	17.95	_____
_____	Nail the Resume!	17.95	_____
_____	Resume, Application, and Letter Tips for People With Hot and Not-so-Hot Backgrounds	17.95	_____
_____	Resume Magic	18.95	_____
_____	Resumes for Dummies	18.99	_____
_____	Savvy Resume Writer	12.95	_____
_____	Winning Letters That Overcome Barriers to Employment	17.95	_____

Networking and Social Media

QTY.	TITLES	PRICE	TOTAL
_____	Branding Yourself	$24.99	_____
_____	Dig Your Well Before You're Thirsty	16.95	_____
_____	How to Find a Job on LinkedIn, Facebook, Twitter, and Google+	20.00	_____
_____	How to Work a Room	15.99	_____
_____	Job Searching With Social Media for Dummies	19.99	_____
_____	Knock 'Em Dead Social Networking	15.99	_____
_____	LinkedIn for Dummies	24.99	_____
_____	The Little Black Book of Connections	19.95	_____
_____	Make Your Contacts Count	14.95	_____
_____	Networking for People Who Hate Networking	16.95	_____
_____	Never Eat Alone	27.00	_____
_____	The Power Formula for LinkedIn Success	16.95	_____
_____	Self-Promotion for Introverts	22.00	_____
_____	Social Media Job Search Workbook	39.00	_____
_____	Social Networking for Career Success	20.00	_____
_____	Social Networking for Introverts	22.00	_____
_____	Work the Pond	16.95	_____

Small Talk

QTY.	TITLES	PRICE	TOTAL
_____	The Fine Art of Small Talk	$18.00	_____
_____	How to Be a People Magnet	18.00	_____
_____	How to Make People Like You in 90 Seconds or Less	11.95	_____
_____	How to Start a Conversation and Make Friends	15.00	_____
_____	How to Talk So People Listen	12.99	_____
_____	How to Talk to Anyone	16.95	_____
_____	Talking to Yourself	9.95	_____

Storytelling

QTY.	TITLES	PRICE	TOTAL
_____	LinkedIn: Tell Your Story, Land the Job	$12.99	_____
_____	Tell Me About Yourself	24.95	_____
_____	Tell Stories Get Hired	19.95	_____

QTY.	TITLES	PRICE	TOTAL
Interviewing			
_____	101 Dynamite Questions to Ask At Your Job Interview	$13.95	_____
_____	101 Great Answers to the Toughest Interview Questions	12.99	_____
_____	Best Answers to 202 Job Interview Questions	17.95	_____
_____	I Can't Believe They Asked Me That!	17.95	_____
_____	Job Interview Tips for People With Not-So-Hot Backgrounds	14.95	_____
_____	Knock 'Em Dead Job Interviews	14.95	_____
_____	Nail the Job Interview	17.95	_____
_____	Savvy Interviewing	10.95	_____
_____	Sweaty Palms	13.95	_____
_____	Win the Interview, Win the Job	15.95	_____
_____	You Should Hire Me!	15.95	_____
Salary Negotiations			
_____	Get a Raise in 7 Days	$16.95	_____
_____	Give Me More Money!	17.95	_____
_____	Salary Negotiation Tips for Professionals	16.95	_____
Job Keeping and Revitalization			
_____	How to Be a Star At Work	$15.00	_____
_____	Love 'Em or Lose 'Em	24.95	_____
_____	The One Thing You Need to Know	29.95	_____
_____	Overcoming 101 More Employment Barriers	19.95	_____
_____	What Your Boss Doesn't Tell You Until It's Too Late	13.95	_____
_____	Who Gets Promoted, Who Doesn't, and Why	14.95	_____
Attitude, Motivation, and Inspiration			
_____	7 Habits of Highly Effective People	$17.00	_____
_____	17 Lies That Are Holding You Back	19.99	_____
_____	30 Lessons for Living	16.00	_____
_____	100 Ways to Motivate Yourself	15.99	_____
_____	The Art of Doing	16.00	_____
_____	Attitude Is Everything	16.99	_____
_____	Awaken the Giant Within	17.99	_____
_____	Breaking the Habit of Being Yourself	16.95	_____
_____	Change Your Attitude	16.99	_____
_____	Change Your Thinking, Change Your Life	22.00	_____
_____	Create Your Own Future	21.00	_____
_____	Do What You Love, the Money Will Follow	17.00	_____
_____	The Element: How Finding Y our Passion Changes Everything	16.00	_____
_____	Finding Your Own North Star	15.00	_____
_____	Get the Life You Want	19.95	_____
_____	Goals!	19.95	_____
_____	How to Win Friends and Influence People	16.95	_____
_____	Magic of Thinking Big	15.99	_____
_____	The Power of Habit	16.00	_____
_____	The Power of Positive Thinking	15.99	_____
_____	The Purpose-Driven Life	16.99	_____
_____	Reinventing Your Life	17.00	_____
_____	The Secret	23.95	_____

QTY.	TITLES	PRICE	TOTAL
_____	The Success Principles	19.99	_____
_____	Think and Grow Rich	18.95	_____
_____	What Should I Do With My Life?	18.00	_____
_____	What You're Really Meant to Do	27.00	_____
_____	Wishcraft: How to Get What You Really Want	16.00	_____

Reimagining a Life With Purpose

QTY.	TITLES	PRICE	TOTAL
_____	Claiming Your Place At the Fire	$16.95	_____
_____	From Age-ing to Sage-ing	15.00	_____
_____	Life Reimagined: Discovering Your New Life Possibilities	16.95	_____
_____	Man's Search for Meaning	9.99	_____
_____	The Power of Purpose	17.95	_____
_____	Repacking Your Bags	17.95	_____
_____	Something to Live For	16.95	_____
_____	Your Best Life Ever	21.99	_____
_____	Your Life Calling: Reimagining the Rest of Your Life	16.00	_____

Mindfulness

QTY.	TITLES	PRICE	TOTAL
_____	The Gifts of Imperfection	$14.95	_____
_____	Mindfulness: A Practical Guide to Awakening	25.95	_____
_____	Mindfulness for Beginners	21.95	_____
_____	Mindfulness for Dummies	26.99	_____
_____	The Mindfulness Solution	16.95	_____
_____	One-Minute Mindfulness	15.95	_____
_____	The Power of Now	15.00	_____
_____	Super Brain	15.00	_____
_____	Thrive	26.00	_____

Personal Finance

QTY.	TITLES	PRICE	TOTAL
_____	9 Steps to Financial Freedom	$15.99	_____
_____	Money Book for the Young, Fabulous, and Broke	16.00	_____
_____	The Truth About Money	21.95	_____

Ex-Offenders and Re-Entry Success

QTY.	TITLES	PRICE	TOTAL
_____	99 Days to Re-Entry Success Journal	$4.95	_____
_____	Best Jobs for Ex-Offenders	11.95	_____
_____	Best Resumes and Letters for Ex-Offenders	19.95	_____
_____	The Ex-Offender's 30/30 Job Solution	11.95	_____
_____	The Ex-Offender's Job Interview Guide	11.95	_____
_____	The Ex-Offender's New Job Finding and Survival Guide	19.95	_____
_____	The Ex-Offender's Quick Job Hunting Guide	11.95	_____
_____	The Ex-Offender's Re-Entry Assistance Directory	29.95	_____
_____	The Ex-Offender's Re-Entry Success Guide	11.95	_____

Addictions

QTY.	TITLES	PRICE	TOTAL
_____	A to Z of Addictions and Addictive Behaviors	$19.95	_____
_____	The Addiction Workbook	21.95	_____
_____	The Addictive Personality	15.95	_____
_____	Addictive Thinking	15.95	_____
_____	Alcoholics Anonymous: Big Book	14.95	_____
_____	Alcoholism and Addiction Cure	15.95	_____

QTY.	TITLES	PRICE	TOTAL
_____	Breaking Addiction	14.99	_____
_____	Denial Is Not a River in Egypt	13.95	_____
_____	Ending Addiction for Good	14.95	_____
_____	A Gentle Path Through the Twelve Steps	18.95	_____
_____	How to Get Sober and Stay Sober	14.95	_____
_____	How to Quite Drugs for Good!	16.95	_____
_____	The Recovery Book	17.95	_____
_____	Sex, Drugs, Gambling, and Chocolate	16.95	_____
_____	Sober But Stuck	15.95	_____
_____	Stop the Chaos	15.95	_____

Anger and Conflict

QTY.	TITLES	PRICE	TOTAL
_____	Anger and Conflict in the Workplace	$14.95	_____
_____	The Anger Workbook	14.95	_____
_____	Angry Men	14.95	_____
_____	Angry Women	14.95	_____
_____	Beyond Anger: A Guide for Men	15.99	_____
_____	Controlling People	15.99	_____
_____	Of Course You're Angry	14.95	_____

Learning Disabilities and Mental Health

QTY.	TITLES	PRICE	TOTAL
_____	ADD/ADHD Checklist	$16.95	_____
_____	Bipolar Disorder	15.95	_____
_____	Complete Learning Disabilities Handbook	34.95	_____
_____	Delivered From Distraction	16.00	_____
_____	Driven to Distraction	15.95	_____
_____	Feeling Good Handbook	26.00	_____
_____	The Gift of Dyslexia	16.95	_____
_____	Learning Outside the Lines	15.99	_____
_____	Overcoming Dyslexia	17.95	_____
_____	Surviving Manic Depression	19.95	_____
_____	Taking Charge of ADHD	19.95	_____
_____	You Mean I'm Not Lazy, Stupid, or Crazy?	19.00	_____

Start and Manage a Business

QTY.	TITLES	PRICE	TOTAL
_____	$100 Startup	$23.00	_____
_____	101 Small Business Ideas for Under $5,000	32.00	_____
_____	The $100,000 Entrepreneur	19.95	_____
_____	Business Plans Kit for Dummies (with CD-ROM)	34.99	_____
_____	Six-Week Start-Up	21.95	_____
_____	Small Business Start-Up Kit	29.99	_____
_____	Start Your Own Business	24.95	_____

Special Value Kits

QTY.	TITLES	PRICE	TOTAL
_____	Discover What You're Best At Kit	$435.95	_____
_____	Job Finding With Social Media and Technology Kit	282.95	_____
_____	Learning From Successes and Failures Kit	1,059.95	_____
_____	Mindfulness for Refocusing Your Life Kit	297.95	_____
_____	New Attitudes, Goals, and Motivations Kit	411.95	_____
_____	New Military-to-Civilian Transition Kit	653.95	_____

QTY.	TITLES	PRICE	TOTAL
_____	Overcoming Employment Barriers Kit	124.95	_____
_____	Overcoming Self-Defeating Behaviors and Bouncing Back Kit	245.95	_____
_____	Reimagining Life: Discovering Your Meaning and Purpose	203.95	_____
_____	Start Your Own Business Kit	316.95	_____
_____	Tony Robbins "Transform Your Life" Collection	189.95	_____

DVD Programs

QTY.	TITLES	PRICE	TOTAL
_____	135 Interview Answers	$169.95	_____
_____	175 Resume Secrets	169.95	_____
_____	207 Interview Techniques	169.95	_____
_____	Barriers to Communication and How to Overcome Them	129.95	_____
_____	Careers in the Nonprofit Sector	129.95	_____
_____	Common Job Interview Mistakes	99.95	_____
_____	Digital Communication Skills	129.95	_____
_____	E-Networking for Jobs	129.95	_____
_____	Get Hired and Go	599.95	_____
_____	Getting the Job You Really Want	995.00	_____
_____	Job Seeker: Interview Do's and Don'ts	169.95	_____
_____	Navigating the World of Social Media	108.00	_____
_____	Resumes: A How-to Guide	99.95	_____
_____	Soft Skills in the Workplace	149.95	_____
_____	STEM Careers in Two Years	389.95	_____
_____	What Will I Say at the Interview?	129.95	_____
_____	You're Fired!	149.00	_____

TERMS: Individuals must prepay; approved accounts are billed net 30 days. All orders under $100.00 should be prepaid.

RUSH ORDERS: fax, call, or email for more information on any special shipping arrangements and charges.

SUBTOTAL		_____
Virginia residents add 6% sales tax		_____
California residents add ____% sales tax		_____
Shipping ($5 +8% of SUBTOTAL)		_____
TOTAL ORDER		_____

Bill To:

Name_____ Title _____
Address_____
City _____ State/Zip _____
Phone (   )_____ (daytime)
Email_____

Ship To: (if different from "Bill To;" include street del. address).

Name_____ Title _____
Address_____
City _____ State/Zip _____
Phone (   )_____ (daytime)
Email_____

PAYMENT METHOD: ❑ **Purchase Order** #_____ (attach or fax with this order form)

❑ **Check** – Make payable to IMPACT PUBLICATIONS

❑ **Credit Card**: ❑ Visa ❑ MasterCard ❑ AMEX ❑ Discover

Card #													Expiration Date		
Signature							Name on Card (print)								

The Best Keywords for Resumes, Letters, and Interviews

Powerful Words and Phrases for Landing Great Jobs! (2nd Edition)

Wendy S. Enelow and Louise Kursmark, Master Resume Writers

Copyright © April 2016

192 pages. 7" x 10"

ISBN 978-1-57023-388-3 (paperback)

ISBN 978-1-57023-389-0 (eBook)

Business/Careers

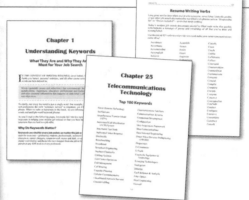

Quantity Discounts

Copies	Discount	Per Unit Cost	Bulk		Purchases*
1-9	0%	$19.95	1 copy	=	$19.95
10-24 copies	20%	($15.96)	10 copies	=	$159.60
25-49 copies	30%	($13.98)	25 copies	=	$349.25
50-99 copies	40%	($11.97)	50 copies	=	$598.50
100-499 copies	50%	($9.98)	100 copies	=	$998.00
500-999 copies	55%	($8.98)	500 copies	=	$4,490.00
1,000-4,999 copies	60%	($7.98)	1,000 copies	=	$7,980.00

*Prices do not include shipping

ORDERS AND QUANTITY DISCOUNTS:

1-800-361-1055 or www.impactpublications.com

Overcoming Barriers to Employment Kit

NEW!

#4474 Focusing on major employment barriers, this resource collection reveals inside strategies for overcoming each barrier. They address major employability issues for those lacking sufficient work experience, education, skills, motivation, direction, and drive as well as those dealing with a variety of behavioral issues, such as job hopping, anger, substance abuse, negative attitudes, time gaps, and incarceration. Can purchase separately. **SPECIAL: $583.95 for all 17 resources.**

BOOKS

- *12 Bad Habits That Hold Good People Back* ($15.95)
- *95 Mistakes Job Seekers Make and How to Avoid Them* ($13.95)
- *Attitude is Everything* ($16.99)
- *The Ex-Offender's New Job Finding and Survival Guide* ($19.95)
- *Job Hunting Tips for People With Hot and Not-So-Hot Backgrounds* ($17.95)
- *Job Interview Tips for People With Not-So-Hot Backgrounds* ($14.95)
- *No One is Unemployable* ($29.95)
- *No One Will Hire Me!* ($15.95)
- *Now, Discover Your Strengths* ($32.00)

- *Overcoming 101 More Barriers to Employment* ($19.95)
- *Overcoming Barriers to Employment Success* ($17.95)
- *Overcoming Employment Barriers* ($19.95)
- *The Quick 30/30 Job Solution* ($14.95)
- *Winning Letters That Overcome Barriers to Employment* ($17.95)

DVDs and Instruments

- *Barriers to Communication and How to Overcome Them* ($129.95)
- *Barriers to Employment Success* ($149.00)
- *Barriers to Employment Success Inventory* ($63.95 for package of 25)

The Ultimate Habit-Change Kit:

Transforming Yourself Through Willpower, Self-Control, and a New Mindset

NEW!

#5193 A fabulous new cutting-edge kit. Much of success and happiness in life centers on certain habits or routines that require little or no decision-making on our part. Such auto-behavior, whether good or bad, frees us up to focus on other aspects of living. This personal growth kit, which includes the latest insights on willpower, self-control, mindset, stress, and resilience, pulls together some of the finest resources for understanding habits and developing effective techniques for both breaking debilitating habits and acquiring productive habits. Can purchase separately. **SPECIAL: $579.95 for all 32 books.**

- *7 Habits of Highly Effective Families* ($16.99)
- *7 Habits of Highly Effective People* ($17.00)
- *12 Bad Habits That Hold Good People Back* ($15.95)
- *The 8th Habit* ($16.95)
- *Abundance Now: Amplify Your Life and Achieve Prosperity Today* ($25.99)
- *The Achievement Habit: Stop Wishing, Start Doing, and Take Command of Your Life* ($27.99)
- *The Art of Good Habits* ($16.99)
- *Better Than Before: What I Learned About Making and Breaking Habits* ($16.00)
- *Bouncing Back: Rewiring Your Brain for Maximum Resilience and Well-Being* ($17.95)
- *Breaking the Habit of Being Yourself: How to Lose Your Mind and Create a New One* ($16.99)
- *Changing for Good* ($14.99)
- *Eat That Frog! 21 Great Ways to Stop Procrastinating and Get More Done in Less Time* ($15.95)
- *Four Seconds* ($25.99)
- *The Gifts of Imperfection* ($15.95)
- *Habit Change Workbook* ($27.95)
- *Habits of a Happy Brain* ($15.99)
- *How to Win Friends and Influence People* ($16.00)

- *Life-Changing Magic of Tidying Up* ($16.99)
- *Making Good Habits, Breaking Bad Habits: 14 New Behaviors That Will Energize Your Life* ($15.00)
- *Making Habits, Breaking Habits: Why We Do Things, Why We Don't* ($15.99)
- *The Marshmallow Test: Mastering Self-Control* ($29.00)
- *Mindset: The New Psychology of Success* ($16.00)
- *The Power of Habit* ($16.00)
- *Primary Greatness: The 12 Levers of Success* ($24.95)
- *Quiet: The Power of Introverts in a World That Can't Stop Talking* ($16.00)
- *Rewire: Change Your Brain to Break Bad Habits, Overcome Addictions, Conquer Self-Destructive Behavior* ($16.00)
- *The Success Principles* ($19.99)
- *Thinking, Fast and Slow* ($16.00)
- *This Year I Will...* ($16.95)
- *The Upside of Stress: Why Stress is Good for You, and How to Get Good at It* ($26.95)
- *Willpower: Rediscovering the Greatest Human Strength* ($17.00)
- *The Willpower Instinct* ($17.00)

ORDERS: 1.800.361.1055 or www.impactpublications.com

Job Finding With Social Media and Technology Kit

#8471 Update your career library by getting the latest inside scoop on how to conduct a powerful job search using social media and technology. Each book is filled with useful strategies and examples. Can purchase each separately. **SPECIAL: $282.95 for all 14 books.**

- *The 2-Hour Job Search* ($12.99)
- *Branding Yourself* ($24.99)
- *Guerrilla Marketing for Job Hunters 3.0* ($21.95)
- *How to Find a Job on LinkedIn, Facebook, Twitter, and Google +* ($20.00)
- *Job Searching With Social Media for Dummies* ($19.99)
- *Knock 'Em Dead Social Networking* ($15.99)
- *LinkedIn for Dummies* ($24.99)
- *The Panic Free Job Search* ($15.99)
- *The Power Formula for LinkedIn Success* ($16.95)
- *Resumes for Dummies* ($18.99)
- *The Social Media Job Search Workbook* ($49.00)
- *Social Networking for Career Success* ($20.00)
- *The Web 2.0 Job Finder* ($15.99)
- *What Color Is Your Parachute?* ($19.99)

Discover What You're Best at Kit

#3013 Finding the right job and career path requires assessment of interests, skills, and goals before all else. These 22 resources are jam-packed with the tools to help you identify your major strengths. **SPECIAL: $441.95 for complete kit!**

BOOKS

- *Career Match* ($15.00)
- *Change Your Thinking, Change Your Life* ($22.00)
- *Discover the Best Jobs for You* ($15.95)
- *Discover What You're Best At* ($15.99)
- *Do What You Are* ($18.99)
- *The Element* ($16.00)
- *Everything Career Tests Book* ($15.99)
- *Finding Your Own North Star* ($15.00)
- *Gifts Differing* ($18.95)
- *Go Put Your Strengths to Work* ($16.00)
- *Goals!* ($19.95)
- *I Don't Know What I Want, But I Know It's Not This* ($15.00)
- *I'm Not Crazy, I'm Just Not You* ($19.95)
- *Pathfinder* ($17.99)
- *Strengths Finder* ($29.95)
- *What Color Is Your Parachute Workbook* ($12.99)

- *What Should I Do With My Life?* ($18.00)
- *What Type Am I?* ($17.00)
- *What's Your Type of Career?* ($24.95)
- *Wishcraft* ($16.00)

INSTRUMENTS

- *Barriers to Employment Success Inventory* (set of 25, $63.95)
- *Career Exploration Inventory* (set of 25, $60.95)

Ace the Interview and Salary Negotiation Kit

#8688 The job interview and salary negotiation are the most important steps in a job search. Here's the ultimate collection of relevant books and DVDs. **SPECIAL: $464.95 for all 13 resources.**

BOOKS

- *101 Dynamite Questions to Ask at Your Job Interview* ($13.95)
- *Ace The IT Job Interview* ($24.95)
- *Best Answers to 202 Job Interview Questions* ($17.95)
- *Give Me More Money!* ($17.95)
- *I Can't Believe They Asked Me That!* ($17.95)
- *Job Interview Tips for People With Not-So-Hot Backgrounds* ($14.95)
- *Job Interviews For Dummies* ($17.99)
- *Negotiating Your Salary: How to Make $1,000 a Minute* ($15.95)
- *Sweaty Palms* ($13.95)
- *Win the Interview, Win the Job* ($15.95)
- *You Should Hire Me!* ($15.95)

DVDs

- *Good First Impressions* ($149.00)
- *Quick Interview and Salary Negotiation Video* ($149.00)

ORDERS: 1.800.361.1055 or www.impactpublications.com